T0065153

The Art of Public Service:

Changing How We Think About Bureaucracy and Its Impacts

Robert Choi

ARCHWAY
PUBLISHING

Archway Publishing books may be ordered through booksellers or by contacting:

Archway Publishing
1663 Liberty Drive
Bloomington, IN 47403
www.archwaypublishing.com
844-669-3957

ISBN: 978-1-6657-5363-0 (sc)
ISBN: 978-1-6657-5364-7 (e)

Library of Congress Control Number: 2023922469

Print information available on the last page.

Archway Publishing rev. date: 11/28/2023

CONTENTS

ACKNOWLEDGMENTS

At the heart of this book's creation lies a profound gratitude to Major Willie Merkerson, Jr., DSC, US Army (Retired), whose influence extends beyond the professional guidance expected of a superior. To the best boss I ever had: your leadership was the compass that navigated me through challenges, your wisdom a beacon that dispelled the fog of uncertainty. But more importantly, perhaps in ways that have gone unsaid until now, you have been a father-figure and a steadfast role model in my life. Your unwavering integrity, courage, and compassion have quietly shaped my path, and it is with deep respect and affection that I dedicate the effort of this work to you. Your exemplary life has been a masterclass in honor and humanity, and for that, I am eternally grateful.

ABOUT THE BOOK

The Art of Public Service: Changing How We Think About Bureaucracy and Its Impacts is a transformative guide that redefines our perception of bureaucracy. Delving deep into the heart of government, Choi unravels the human element often lost amidst the maze of procedures and paperwork. This book is not just a narrative; it's a journey canvassing the lives of those who serve, highlighting the emotional labor, ethical challenges, and personal triumphs inherent in public service.

Each chapter skillfully weaves personal stories with practical strategies, offering a unique perspective on navigating the bureaucratic system. From uncovering the emotional toll of paperwork in "The Weight of Paperwork" to exploring moral dilemmas in "The Ethical Compass," Choi's insightful analysis and heartfelt storytelling illuminate the soul behind the bureaucracy.

Innovative and inspiring, *The Art of Public Service* goes beyond the conventional. It's a call to embrace vulnerability in leadership, as seen in "Leading with Heart," and to integrate personal experiences into policy-making in "Policy with a Pulse." The book culminates in a powerful vision for the future in "Reimagining the Future" and "Transformative Leadership," urging readers to craft their legacy within the governmental landscape.

Accompanied by practical Section Coaching, including resources on self-care and advocacy, this book is an essential read for students of government, government employees, elected officials, and anyone interested in the intersection of personal and professional growth and public service. Robert Choi's work is more than a book; it's a movement towards a more empathetic, efficient, and ethical government. Join the journey and redefine what it means to serve.

ABOUT THE AUTHOR(S)

Robert Choi is an author deeply dedicated to improving government efficiency and effectiveness through a people-centric approach. His ability to create collaborative work environments has been recognized at the Central Intelligence Agency and by the Office of Director of National Intelligence. Serving as the Deputy Chief of HR at New York's Metropolitan Transit Authority, Robert played a crucial role in guiding the organization through the challenges of the COVID-19 pandemic, implementing innovative technologies to enhance operations. Beyond his impactful government service, Robert continues to work as an executive coach and consultant to drive meaningful change and innovation across various sectors with a focus on creating powerful and practical solutions. He holds an MA in Government from Johns Hopkins University and a BA in Political Science from Columbia University.

AUTHOR'S NOTE

This book is designed to reflect the complexities and nuances of public service and leadership, and it is the author's hope that the narratives will resonate with readers and encourage reflection on the profound impact of authenticity and integrity in public life. It is intended to provide information and insights based on the author's experience and research in the fields of public service and leadership. While the book discusses concepts related to mental health, emotional well-being, and personal development, it is not a substitute for professional mental health advice, diagnosis, or treatment. The author is not a licensed mental health professional. Readers are encouraged to consult with qualified health care professionals for any mental health concerns or conditions. The recommendations and opinions expressed in this book are for informational purposes only and should not be considered as medical or psychological advice.

The scenarios, stories, and examples included in this book are provided to illustrate concepts and should not be interpreted as specific advice for individual situations. The author and publisher disclaim any liability arising directly or indirectly from the use or application of any information contained in this book. Additionally, the stories contained within this book are a tapestry of narratives inspired by real-life events and experiences. Names and identifying details have been changed to protect the privacy of individuals, except in cases where public figures are being discussed. Any resemblance to actual persons, living or dead, or actual events is purely coincidental, except where explicitly stated.

Readers should be aware that the stories herein, while rooted in real-life experiences, have been filtered through the lens of the author's perspective and have been shaped, in part, for thematic resonance and coherence. They are intended to inform, inspire, and provoke thought, rather than serve as documentary accounts of events or as a historical record.

The Call to Public Service

Public service is a vast and variegated canvas, where the myriad hues of individual dedication contribute to a portrait of collective progress. This canvas stretches through the corridors of time, encompassing the ancient footprints of the first civil servants who etched laws in stone, to today's policymakers drafting legislation that echoes through the digital age. It's where the heartbeats of countless unsung heroes resonate with the quiet hum of progress, their decisions and deeds the invisible hand guiding society's evolution. To heed this call is to walk a path paved by pioneers and visionaries, a path that, though often shrouded in the penumbra of bureaucracy, is lit by the lantern of purpose, profoundly impactful in the shaping of our world.

This calling transcends the transactional nature of a job. It is a noble vocation that demands a unique blend of sacrifice, courage, and a steadfast commitment to the common good. Like a clarion call, it resonates in moments of lucidity, cutting through the clamor of everyday life, compelling one to recognize the power and privilege of serving their fellow citizens. It is a profound realization that within the mechanisms of governance lies the potential to affect real change—to grease the wheels of progress, to mold the lives of future generations, and to foster communities where hope can flourish unfettered.

The narratives of those who have heeded this call are as kaleidoscopic as the society they endeavor to serve. For some, it was the sight of inequity and the desire to right what is wrong that fanned the embers of their resolve. Others were beckoned by the luminescence of possibility—the chance to improve communities, to weave equity into the fabric of our institutions, to champion kindness in the face of adversity. It is this very diversity of inspiration that infuses the lifeblood of democracy, each drop a testament to the conviction that the singular voice of one can crescendo into the symphony of many.

To serve the public is to pledge oneself to a journey of perpetual learning and adaptation. It is to engage with the labyrinth of policies and procedures with a spirit not of forbearance but of enthusiasm, viewing them not as barriers but as the scaffolding upon which society's voice can resonate, its needs be met, and its collective dreams be realized. Within the perceived rigidity of bureaucracy lies a pulsating spirit of potential, a bedrock upon which the seeds of transformational change can be sown—the very essence of hope itself.

The true heartbeat of public service lies in its people—those who dedicate their lives to serve and those who are the beneficiaries of this service. Each day, in nations and neighborhoods around the globe, public servants emerge as the architects of our future, the stewards of our environment, the sentinels of our safety, and the enablers of our day-to-day lives. Their contributions, often unheralded and underappreciated, are not for personal acclaim or financial gain but for the satisfaction of a promise fulfilled—a promise to contribute to a legacy greater than oneself.

Yet, the call to public service carries with it its own set of formidable challenges. It demands resilience in the face of adversity, patience against the seemingly glacial pace of change, and creativity in weaving solutions through the intricate web of governance. It is a call that asks for an unyielding adherence to one's values, an unwavering sense of integrity, and a commitment to dedication even in the face of overwhelming odds.

This call is also an open invitation—an invitation to become part of a lineage of service, to join a community of dedicated individuals who grasp the weight of their responsibilities as keenly as they relish the buoyancy of their collective achievements. It is an invitation to etch one's name in the annals of history, to contribute to the narrative of nation-building, community shaping, and policy forging.

As we venture through the chapters of this book, we will journey through the personal stories that chart the landscape of public service. These narratives will lay bare the inner workings of government through the eyes of those who have committed themselves to the cause of public service, providing insights and inspirations for those who might, in turn, heed the call themselves. The call to public service is both a privilege and a responsibility. As we turn the page to explore the world of public service, let us do so with a sense of reverence for its storied past, a robust engagement with its dynamic present, and an unwavering hope for its promising future.

Personal Journeys: Why We Serve

Every individual who answers the call to public service embarks on a journey unique to their vision, values, and virtues. These personal voyages are rarely charted in advance; they are the sum of experiences, aspirations, and often an innate desire to contribute to the greater good. There's an inherent beauty in the unpredictability of these paths, where each twist and turn is guided by a moral compass pointing towards service beyond oneself. In these personal stories, we uncover the profound 'whys' that anchor us to the sometimes turbulent, often rewarding sea of public service. They speak to us in silent reverberations, urging us to forge ahead when the tides grow rough.

When we pause to listen to the stories of why we serve, we often hear a recurring theme of pivotal moments—instances where the abstract became personal, where societal issues touched our lives or the lives of those we love. These are the defining junctures that draw a line in the sand of our existence, challenging us to step over into the domain of active citizenship. For some, it was witnessing the struggles of a community battling poverty or illness, where empathy transformed into a lifelong mission. For others, it was the realization that policy isn't just penned text, but the very brush with which we paint the contours of society's future, an epiphany that what is written down in law has the power to uplift or to oppress, to include or to marginalize.

For the environmental lawyer, for example, it may have been childhood days spent in awe of nature's majesty, a connection so deep that protecting the environment became synonymous with protecting a part of themselves. It's in the crisp air of the early morning hikes, the rustle of leaves, and the chirp of birds where the commitment was fostered. For the urban planner, it might have been the complexities of their bustling neighborhood, where the confluence of culture, commerce, and community sparked a desire to design cities that celebrate diversity and foster connection. It's a belief in the power of place to shape lives and in the importance of planning spaces that enable communities to thrive in harmony. The healthcare administrator works tirelessly not only because of a professional mandate, but because of a vision where access to health is a universal treasure, not a lottery of birth, where every individual is guaranteed the right to wellness.

The stories are as varied as they are inspiring. A teacher turned policymaker who, after years in the classroom, sought the levers of power to revamp an education system that left too many behind, driven by memories of bright eyes dimmed by inequity. A veteran who, after serving abroad, returned to serve at home, channeling discipline and leadership into community development, inspired by the camaraderie and sense of purpose found in shared service. A technocrat, moved by the digital divide's widening chasm, rallying for a future where technology bridges gaps rather than deepens them, motivated by the conviction that in the digital age, connectivity is a right, not a privilege.

Public servants often speak of a sense of responsibility, a feeling that the skills and privileges they possess are not just personal assets but communal tools meant to build, uplift, and reform. They carry the profound understanding that their abilities are not meant to be hoarded but shared generously, like a beacon guiding ships to shore. There is an understanding that to whom much is given, much is expected—a principle that transforms talent and knowledge into the currency of change.

Embedded within these journeys is the acknowledgment of the intrinsic challenges that come with the territory of public service—the long hours, the complex problems, the often-glacial pace of progress. Yet, these challenges are willingly embraced because the call to serve is accompanied by an enduring belief in possibility, in the potential for incremental actions to culminate in monumental shifts. It is the knowledge that through the often imperceptible daily grind, legacies are built one decision, one policy, one act of service at a time. The victories are sometimes silent, the triumphs unnoticed, but the impact is immeasurable, echoing through the lives touched by commitment and care.

Why we serve is also about the people, about faces and stories that linger in the mind long after the office lights dim. It's about the grandmother who can afford her medication because a policy was changed, the immigrant family that finds belonging in a new community because a law was passed, the child who dreams bigger because a program, a policy, or a person in public service believed they could. It's in these individual stories where we find the fuel to continue, the reminders of the flesh-and-blood impact of seemingly distant decisions.

Why we serve is as much a reflection on personal values as it is on societal impact. Public servants are mirrors reflecting their communities' needs, hopes, and challenges, often setting aside personal gain for public benefit. These individuals embody the concept of the public trust, standing as stewards of the collective good. In the myriad stories of why we serve, we find common threads of empathy, justice, and an unshakeable conviction that our shared futures are worth the toil.

The ensuing chapters will unravel these threads, exploring the depths of personal commitment to public service. As we walk through the halls of bureaucracy, we will discover that within the hearts of those who serve, lies the pulse of public life, the sincere effort to leave an imprint for good, to serve not because one has to, but because one is compelled by something greater—a call that resonates with one's very being. It's a resonance felt in the quiet moments, the shared glances, the firm handshakes, and the shared resolve to press on in the

CHAPTER 1

The Soul of Bureaucracy

1.1. Beyond Red Tape: Finding Meaning in Procedure

In the grand labyrinth of government, where each corridor is fortified by
the rules and edicts that are the lifeblood of order, it's not uncommon for
the spirit of governance to be overshadowed by its structure. The concept
of 'red tape' has become synonymous with a bureaucratic quagmire, a
symbol of inefficiency and frustration.[1] Yet, within this complex network
lies a deeper narrative—one that sees the alignment of procedure with
purpose, and policy with the pulse of human ambition. When we begin
to perceive procedural diligence as a vessel for significant reform, we can
rekindle the flame of inspiration that often gets dimmed in the day-to-
day shuffle of papers and permits.

Our journey into the essence of bureaucracy reveals a landscape where
constraints can become catalysts, and the ordered lines of bureaucracy
can be the very threads that weave together a fabric of societal progression.
This evolution hinges on an intrinsic understanding of the foundations
upon which governmental operations are built, viewing each act not
as an isolated demand of compliance but as a chord in a harmonious
symphony of public service. By embracing this perspective, we shift
from enduring the mundane to crafting the exceptional, from enduring
governance to enlivening it.

In reimagining our bond with procedure, we ought to envision each
document and decision as a covenant with the legacy of our civilization.

The deliberate intricacy involved in sculpting policy, the vigilant care in performing administrative tasks—these must be seen as more than obligatory steps. [2] They are, in truth, commitments to a sacred trust bequeathed to us by the public, who expects not just efficiency, but integrity and foresight in the stewardship of their collective well-being. Reflect on this: researchers have quantified the sheer volume of time that businesses dedicate to navigating federal regulations. Such a colossal investment of energy could, at a glance, be deemed an excessive drain on productivity.[3] Yet, if we shift our perspective to see each of these hours as a testament to our dedication to due diligence, clarity, and the upholding of standards that protect and serve the citizenry, we start to appreciate the magnitude of our responsibility.[4] This pivot in perspective underscores our role not as mere functionaries but as gatekeepers of the public good.

The search for significance in procedural tasks necessitates an intellectual and emotional transformation—a reorientation of vision. In healthcare, for example, HIPAA's intricacy can be perceived as cumbersome. However, at its essence, the act is a bulwark defending the sanctity of the patient-provider bond, the confidentiality that nurtures trust, and hence, the quality of care. Within its detailed clauses lies a commitment to honoring the stories and vulnerabilities entrusted to healthcare professionals. By protecting these narratives, we affirm the individual's inherent worth.[5]

Globally, we see nations like Bhutan championing the happiness of their citizens, integrating this ethos into every layer of governmental policy. This demonstrates a profound understanding that the metrics by which we measure our governance profoundly dictate the nature of our procedures and the outcomes they engender. It's a clarion call for the prioritization of empathetic and human-centric approaches within the procedural framework of governance.[6]

Grasping the significance of processes also means acknowledging the might of gradual advancement. In seeking purposeful public service, we recognize that monumental change often stems from modest initiatives. The implementation of comprehensive regulations like those seen in the

Dodd-Frank Act illustrates that careful, methodical policymaking can redirect the course of entire industries towards resilience and fairness, protecting the public from the ramifications of unchecked market behaviors.

Moreover, by embracing the procedural facets of governance, we lay the groundwork for justice and equality. Well-crafted procedures are the embodiment of fairness within a democratic framework, guaranteeing that each individual is held to the same measure of law and ethics, ensuring impartiality and equity. Nevertheless, it's imperative to strike a balance, to remember that our allegiance is to the people and not to the process itself. We must engender a culture where government employees are not only implementers but also innovators, encouraged to refine and reform processes to better serve their purpose without diminishing their rigor or effectiveness.

As we seek meaning within the procedural landscape, data stands as our guiding star. Analytical examination of administrative procedures can reveal underperformance and spotlight how systems either facilitate or fail to serve society. Innovative methodologies like process mining enable us to dissect and comprehend the actual workflows, identifying inefficiencies and paving the way for transformative simplification.

Looking to the horizon, it is our collective responsibility to shift the paradigm of bureaucracy. Let us envision our rules and regulations not as constraints but as welcomes, as pathways to participation in the grand pursuit of governance. By infusing each procedure with intention and each policy with zeal, we not only enhance our service but also elevate our vocation as public servants. In this endeavor, each regulatory action becomes a stride towards crafting a more equitable and noble union.

1.2. Stories from the Inside: The Unsung Heroes of Public Service

Sandra's daily encounters at the county clerk's office might not make the evening news, but they are woven into the fabric of her community's narrative. Her position may be characterized by the unremarkable churn of bureaucracy, yet Sandra operates at the junction of personal milestones and administrative processes. Observing the impatience and sometimes frustration of those waiting in line, Sandra saw not just individuals in a queue but stories waiting to unfold, moments being missed, and life passing by in the dull hum of routine. She channeled this empathy into action, overhauling the registration system with a blend of technological savvy and an intuitive understanding of workflow management. The impact of her initiative resonated beyond efficiency metrics—it was measured in the smiles of parents more swiftly returning home to cradle their newborns, in the eyes of couples more quickly embarking on marital journeys, and in the solace of families finding more time to comfort each other in mourning. Sandra's commitment to improving the citizen-government interaction exemplifies the profound effect one person's thoughtful innovation can have in turning the wheels of bureaucracy with more grace and less grind.

Sandra's transformation of the county clerk's office into a hub of efficiency and human connection did not happen overnight. It was a meticulous journey marked by keen observation, technological integration, and a profound commitment to service that uplifted the spirit of her community. Her approach was methodical. Sandra first undertook a comprehensive analysis of the existing registration processes. She observed every step, from the moment constituents walked through the door to the completion of their transactions. She took notes, identified bottlenecks, and patiently listened to the grievances and suggestions of the public. Sandra understood that to reform the system, she needed to perceive it through the eyes of those it served.

Armed with data and firsthand accounts, Sandra then crafted a detailed plan to overhaul the registration system. She introduced an online appointment scheduling system, which allowed constituents to reserve their slot, thus eliminating the uncertainty of wait times. She also implemented an automated form-filling system where constituents could pre-fill their details, saving time for both the public and the clerks. Sandra's plan went beyond just the introduction of technology. She redesigned the office layout to create a more welcoming and organized space. She established clear signage and information points to guide constituents through their visit, reducing confusion and the need for repetitive instruction.

Training the staff was a critical component of her plan. Sandra organized workshops to ensure that every employee was adept at using the new technology and understood the new workflow. She fostered an environment of continuous feedback and improvement, where the staff's insights contributed to refining the processes further. Her empathetic leadership and technological savvy culminated in a pilot program within her division. The success of this pilot, measured not just in reduced processing times but also in the heightened morale of both staff and constituents, became the cornerstone of a department-wide transformation.

Sandra's initiative resonated across the organization, prompting a cultural shift towards a service-oriented mindset. The ripple effects were profound – reduced paper waste, expedited services, and an overall enhancement in the quality of interaction between the government and its citizens. By placing people at the heart of the process, Sandra transformed an ordinary bureaucratic procedure into an extraordinary experience of efficiency and connection.

Alex, on the other hand, operates in a realm where numbers narrate the unfolding of public health stories. In the intricate dance of public health management, where data points are the silent sentinels guarding the well-being of a population, Alex's story unfolds—a narrative of preemptive action and analytical acumen. The looming threat of a contagious disease was not merely a professional hurdle; it was a clarion call to which Alex responded with the full might of his expertise. His role transcended the boundaries of his job description, morphing into a civic duty that was both urgent and profound.

Alex's first step was to establish a robust data collection system that could capture real-time health statistics across a range of demographics and regions. He developed a comprehensive database that integrated information from hospitals, clinics, and public health surveys, providing a granular view of the population's health landscape. The data was then meticulously analyzed to identify patterns and trends, allowing Alex to pinpoint areas of vulnerability where an outbreak could wreak the most havoc. Equipped with predictive analytics, Alex harnessed advanced algorithms to forecast the spread of the disease, taking into account variables such as population density, mobility patterns, and the efficacy of existing health interventions. This predictive model was the keystone of his strategy, enabling him to deploy resources with precision and foresight. He collaborated with local healthcare providers, emergency response teams, and policy-makers, providing them with actionable insights that informed their decision-making processes.

Alex's proactive measures included the implementation of targeted vaccination drives in the most susceptible regions, bolstering of medical supplies in anticipation of increased demand, and the dissemination of educational materials to raise public awareness about prevention measures. He also advocated for policy changes that would facilitate faster and more efficient responses to health emergencies, emphasizing the need for agility in public health strategies. In the shadow of potential outbreaks, Alex's work stood as a bulwark against the tides of uncertainty. His efforts ensured that the public health system was not caught off guard but was instead prepared to respond to the threat with a well-orchestrated, evidence-based action plan.

The success of Alex's approach was reflected in the resilience of the health system, which managed to contain the spread of the disease effectively, minimizing its impact on the community. His story exemplifies the potency of analytical skills when coupled with a deep-seated commitment to the public good—a synergy that is essential in the realm of public service where the stakes are nothing less than the health and tranquility of society itself.

Grace's story is one of quiet tenacity against the backdrop of the defense department's colossal structure. In addressing the challenge that Grace faced, we observe a narrative of meticulous analysis and strategic reform, one that encapsulates the essence of ethical stewardship in government. Grace's solution to the problem was not born from a moment of eureka, but from a series of methodical evaluations and calculated actions aimed at reforming the procurement processes within her department.

Grace's first step was to establish a baseline for current spending and efficiency. She pored over countless spreadsheets, tracking down each expenditure to its core justification, mapping out where funds were allocated and identifying areas where waste was evident. Her evenings became consumed with analyzing budget lines, comparing cost allocations against outcomes, and understanding the nuanced regulations that govern fiscal policy within the defense department.

Recognizing that fiscal responsibility begins with transparency, Grace developed a comprehensive audit protocol to assess the department's procurement practices. Her approach included a historical analysis of spending patterns, an evaluation of vendor contracts, and a review of the procurement lifecycle to pinpoint inefficiencies. Her findings were startling yet illuminating, revealing a pattern of redundant spending and missed opportunities for cost savings. Empowered with data, Grace initiated a series of roundtable discussions with key stakeholders, including finance officers, procurement specialists, and department leaders. Her goal was to build a coalition for change, framing her findings not as criticisms but as opportunities for improvement. She presented her data with such compelling narrative force that it became impossible to ignore the need for an overhaul.

The cornerstone of Grace's strategy was the implementation of a centralized digital procurement system. This system was designed to be intuitive and user-friendly, ensuring that all department personnel could access real-time data on vendor contracts, pricing models, and spending limits. It also featured automated alerts for budget overruns and an integrated approval hierarchy to streamline the procurement process.

Grace's proposal for a digital transformation was met with resistance from those accustomed to the status quo. However, her persistent advocacy, bolstered by an undeniable economic case, began to turn the tide. She secured the buy-in from senior leadership by demonstrating how the new system could prevent budget overruns and ensure compliance with financial regulations. The launch of the digital procurement system marked a pivotal moment in the department's history. It wasn't merely a technological upgrade; it was a cultural shift towards fiscal prudence and accountability. Grace's initiative led to a substantial reduction in paper use, aligning the department's practices with its broader environmental commitments.

The impact of the new system was profound. Not only did it reduce the department's environmental footprint, but it also resulted in significant cost savings. In its first year of operation, the digital system cut procurement costs by an estimated 20%, according to a departmental efficiency review. It increased transparency, ensuring that taxpayers' money was spent wisely and in alignment with the nation's defense objectives.

Grace's journey illustrates the transformative power of individual agency within a bureaucratic framework. Her story is a testament to the idea that innovation in government does not always require massive budgets or legislative overhauls; sometimes, it's the result of one person's vision, tenacity, and unwavering commitment to change. Her approach exemplifies how a blend of data analytics, strategic planning, and stakeholder engagement can lead to significant improvements in government efficiency and accountability.

These vignettes collectively illustrate that within the gears of bureaucracy operates a workforce driven by a potent combination of will, dedication, and heart, all committed to the advancement of society. Public servants like Sandra, Alex, and Grace embody the ideals of service, often going above and beyond their job descriptions to ensure that the wheels of government turn not only effectively but also with humanity at their core.

The virtue of these individuals extends beyond their immediate roles; it reaches into the communities they serve, fostering a culture of engagement and responsibility. Such dedication to public service is a cornerstone for the stability and prosperity of society as a whole. It's these everyday acts of heroism and dedication that ensure the enduring strength of the institutions they serve, proving that the most impactful changes often stem from the quietest corners of public service.[7]

Beyond the measurable outcomes of efficiency and innovation lies a more profound narrative — the embodiment of personal virtue in the public realm. According to the U.S. Office of Personnel Management, government employees volunteer at rates more than twice the national average, a statistic that speaks volumes about the intrinsic motivation and ethical fiber of those in public service.[8] These individuals are not merely administrators; they are stewards of civic virtue, imbuing their roles with a sense of mission that transcends their official capacities[9]. Their impact is also quantifiable in the stability and development they provide.

In highlighting these stories, it is crucial to appreciate the symbiotic relationship between personal development and public service. As these servants innovate and excel, they not only advance the institutions they represent but also grow as leaders and problem-solvers. The public sector, with its distinct challenges and opportunities, becomes a crucible for personal evolution.[10] When individuals bring their entire selves — their ingenuity, empathy, and commitment to excellence — to their public roles, the resulting impact is profound and far-reaching.

As we turn the page on these stories, let's carry with us the inspiration they instill. Let's recognize that within every policy drafted, every service rendered, there is the potential for a story of heroism waiting to be told. And, perhaps most importantly, let's acknowledge that in the tapestry of public service, every thread — every individual contribution — is vital to the strength and harmony of the whole.

1.3. Navigating the Maze: Personal Strategies for Dealing with Bureaucratic Challenges

Navigating the bureaucratic maze is akin to embarking on a quest within a sprawling, living entity that is in constant flux, growing new corridors and changing its pathways. To become adept at this navigation, one must first become a student of the system, understanding its intricacies and rationale. This knowledge can be a beacon through the fog of complexity, providing the foresight needed to anticipate and prepare for the hurdles that lie ahead. I have observed countless professionals approach this maze with trepidation, only to emerge as master navigators. Let us unpack the personal strategies that facilitate this transformation.

Firstly, engagement with the system must be proactive. A public servant must immerse themselves in the policies and procedures that define their role. By doing so, they forge their armor against the unexpected. Engage with training opportunities, stay updated on policy changes, and interpret these through the lens of your mission. When you understand the 'why' behind the 'what', the rules become tools rather than obstacles.

Goal setting within this framework is also paramount. Not just any goals, but SMART goals - these act as a compass in your quest. A study by American Psychologist found that clear goal setting is one of the most direct routes to higher performance and motivation. By charting a course with precision, one can navigate the labyrinth of public service with intention and measure the impact of their journey.[11]

Collaboration is your ally in this environment. The bureaucratic structure is a tapestry of expertise, and each thread has its role.[12] Create alliances, find mentors, and engage in communities of practice. These relationships are your guides and your support when you encounter crossroads or barriers. The collective intelligence of your network is an invaluable resource that can help you circumvent long-winded passages and find shortcuts to your objectives.

However, even with the best-laid plans, the maze will shift. New policies, emerging technologies, and societal changes will redraw the paths you've come to know. Adaptability is your virtue here. The ability to pivot, to embrace change, and to innovate within the confines of bureaucracy is an art. It's about finding the space between the lines, where creativity meets compliance.[13]

Remember that every twist and turn is rich with lessons. Keep a detailed log of your endeavors - what decisions led to dead ends, which intuitions led to open doors. This knowledge is a gift that keeps on giving, a map you create not only for yourself but for those who will walk this path after you. Institutions that excel in knowledge management, as highlighted by the IBM Center, are beacons of efficiency and innovation because they harness the collective learning of their people.[14]

It's crucial to celebrate milestones. Recognizing your progress fuels your drive and enkindles your passion. The journey is long and often arduous, but each success is a reminder of why you embarked on this path. A Public Administration study found that celebration of small wins is a critical component of sustained employee engagement and productivity.[15]

In essence, navigating the bureaucratic maze is not a solitary endeavor nor a static one. It is a dynamic journey that requires a balance of knowledge, planning, collaboration, adaptability, reflection, and celebration.

Navigating the bureaucratic maze requires a multifaceted approach, blending knowledge, strategy, and emotional intelligence to turn systemic challenges into opportunities for growth and impact. The personal strategies outlined below are crafted to empower public servants to chart their path through the complex web of governmental structures and processes, transforming potential obstacles into stepping stones towards professional fulfillment and success.

Section Coaching:

Deep Systemic Understanding
The first strategy is the cultivation of an in-depth understanding of the bureaucracy itself. This involves studying the historical context, the intended outcomes of policies and procedures, and the roles of various departments and stakeholders. Knowledge is power, and in the realm of bureaucracy, it is the torchlight that illuminates the often shadowy pathways of the system, allowing for anticipation of challenges and preparation of solutions.

Proactive Engagement
Active engagement is pivotal. Staying abreast of policy changes, participating in training sessions, and maintaining a dialogue with policy-makers turns public servants into vital cogs of the bureaucratic

machine, capable of influencing change from within. Engaging proactively transforms employees from passive participants into dynamic agents of change.

Strategic Goal Setting

Setting strategic, Specific, Measurable, Achievable, Relevant, and Time-bound (SMART) goals provides direction and motivation. These goals act as the coordinates in the complex navigation through the bureaucratic system, offering milestones that mark progress and facilitate assessment and realignment of strategies as required.

Collaborative Networks

Collaboration is the lifeblood of effective navigation through bureaucracy. Building a network of allies across departments enhances one's ability to maneuver through the system. Sharing insights, pooling resources, and collective problem-solving can break down silos, creating a more interconnected and responsive bureaucracy.

Adaptability and Innovation

The ability to adapt to changes within the bureaucracy is a critical skill. Public servants must be ready to pivot in response to new policies, shifts in leadership, or changes in public needs. This agility is complemented by a willingness to innovate, to find new ways of working within the rules that enhance efficiency and effectiveness.

Reflective Practice

Keeping a reflective journal of experiences, challenges, and successes serves as a personal case study, a repository of knowledge that can guide current and future actions. It also acts as a narrative of personal growth within the system, providing a sense of progression and a resource for others to learn from.

Celebration of Progress

Recognizing and celebrating each accomplishment, however small, sustains morale and motivation. Acknowledging the incremental achievements reinforces the sense of purpose and commitment to public service, fueling the drive to continue pushing for excellence within the bureaucratic system.

Personal Agency and Advocacy
Maintaining a sense of personal agency within the bureaucracy is empowering. Advocating for oneself, setting personal professional standards, and seeking out opportunities for growth positions public servants as active contributors to the system rather than mere participants.

Workload Management
Effective workload management, including setting realistic expectations, communicating boundaries, and prioritizing tasks, protects against burnout and maintains a focus on quality and impact of work. Balancing professional demands with personal well-being is essential for long-term success in a bureaucratic setting.

Emotional Intelligence
Developing emotional intelligence is integral to navigating bureaucracy. Understanding one's emotions, empathizing with colleagues, and effectively managing interpersonal relationships enhances the ability to work within the system, fostering a supportive and productive work environment.

Leadership Support
Finally, leaders within the bureaucracy play a crucial role in facilitating navigation through the system. They can support their teams by providing resources, recognizing innovation, and advocating for policies that prioritize employee well-being and professional development.

By integrating these strategies, public servants can transform the bureaucratic maze from a daunting labyrinth into a landscape of opportunity. They not only enhance their own capacity to navigate the system but also contribute to the evolution of bureaucracy into a more efficient, responsive, and human-centered entity. By adopting these personal strategies, the maze is not only navigable but can also become a landscape of opportunity - a place where you can leave signposts for those who will navigate these corridors long after you've moved on. Your path through the maze is, in fact, a blueprint for the future - an act of service that extends beyond the immediate and personal to the collective and future transformation of the public sector.

1.4 Finding Meaning in the Machine

Public service is a noble calling, and yet, the very nature of bureaucratic work often leads to an environment riddled with procedural roadblocks and administrative hurdles. These challenges can overshadow the intrinsic motivations that drive individuals to commit to government work in the first place. Within the labyrinthine structures of government, each policy, procedure, and piece of paperwork has a backstory—a reason for its existence.[16] Understanding this context is the first step in finding meaning in the minutiae. Policies are often born out of necessity, shaped by historical precedents, or designed as safeguards against past mistakes. Employees who seek out and comprehend the 'why' behind the 'what' find themselves more engaged and more resilient in the face of bureaucratic challenges.

The sense of purpose in public service can also be reinforced by the impact of one's work on the community. For instance, a city planner drafting zoning regulations is not merely drawing lines on a map but is shaping the lives of residents, influencing the growth of neighborhoods, and protecting the environment. A procurement officer is not just purchasing supplies but is ensuring that firefighters have the tools they need to save lives. By framing their roles within the larger narrative of public good, government workers can connect their daily tasks to the broader mission of their organizations.

However, the path to meaningful work in bureaucracy is not without its trials. Public servants often face the Sisyphean task of pushing against a system resistant to change. In these moments, the narratives of those who have managed to introduce innovation and improvement within the system become beacons of hope. In the most rigid structures, individuals have the power to effect change. When a single, seemingly small efficiency is implemented in a large federal agency, the ripple effect can save countless hours of labor across the organization, translating into significant improvements in service delivery.[17]

The camaraderie that develops between colleagues in the trenches of government work can also be a source of meaning. Shared challenges often give rise to a collective identity and a deep sense of solidarity. The support network that forms within departments or across agencies not only provides emotional sustenance but can also become a powerful force for collective action and reform.[18]

Admittedly, the slow pace of progress and the necessity of navigating through layers of approval can dampen enthusiasm. Here, maintaining a sense of personal agency is key. Government workers who set their own goals, however small, and pursue them with tenacity, often find themselves more satisfied with their careers.[19] This proactive approach—setting benchmarks for personal development, advocating for small-scale improvements, or seeking out creative solutions within the bounds of existing regulations—helps maintain momentum and a positive outlook.

Section Coaching:

To find meaning within the bureaucracy, one must navigate the system with both a strategic mindset and a human-centered approach. This can be achieved through a series of concrete steps that serve to uncover the deeper value and impact of one's work in public service.

Step 1: Educate Yourself About the System
Begin by understanding the history and purpose behind the bureaucratic processes you engage with daily. Research the origins of specific policies and procedures to appreciate their intent and evolution. This knowledge can transform your view of tasks from arbitrary rules to necessary steps in maintaining a fair and orderly society.

Step 2: Connect with the End Result
Make an effort to see where your work goes after it leaves your desk. If possible, follow the lifecycle of a form or policy you've contributed to. Seeing the direct impact of your work on individuals or communities can reinforce the value of your contributions.

Step 3: Personalize the Impact
Shift from viewing those you serve as cases or numbers to recognizing them as individuals with unique stories. Take the opportunity to interact with the public when possible. Understanding their needs and the role your work plays in meeting them can provide a powerful sense of purpose.

Step 4: Innovate Within Your Role
Identify inefficiencies or pain points within your workflow and propose solutions. Small-scale innovations, like improving a filing system or streamlining a process, can lead to significant improvements in service delivery. This proactive approach can create a sense of ownership and satisfaction.

Step 5: Build a Community
Foster relationships with colleagues and create a support network. A collaborative environment can increase job satisfaction and provide a sense of camaraderie. Share successes and work through challenges as a team to create a more meaningful workplace culture.

Step 6: Seek Feedback and Reflect
Regularly solicit feedback on the services you provide and take time to reflect on this input. Adjust your approach based on constructive criticism and recognize the role continuous improvement plays in personal and organizational growth.

Step 7: Set Personal Goals
Define what success looks like for you within the context of your job. Establishing personal benchmarks for what you hope to achieve can help guide your actions and keep you motivated.

Step 8: Celebrate Achievements
Acknowledge and celebrate milestones, both personal and collective. Recognizing progress, no matter how small, can provide a sense of accomplishment and reinforce the importance of your work.

Step 9: Advocate for Change
When you encounter systemic issues, gather data and case studies to advocate for change. Engage in policy discussions and contribute to the dialogue around reform within your agency.

Step 10: Maintain Balance and Self-Care
Recognize the emotional labor involved in public service and prioritize self-care. Establish boundaries to prevent burnout and engage in activities outside of work that replenish your energy and passion.

Step 11: Embrace Lifelong Learning
Continue to expand your skills and knowledge through training, workshops, and education. Lifelong learning keeps you engaged and prepares you for new challenges and opportunities.

Step 12: Mentor and Be Mentored
Participate in mentorship, either as a mentor or mentee. Sharing knowledge and experiences can help others find meaning in their work and can remind you of the broader impact of your own.

These steps offer practical guidance for finding meaning in the bureaucratic work and underscore the importance of a purpose-driven approach to public service. By following these steps, public servants can navigate the system with insight and compassion, making a lasting impact within their roles.

1.5 The Culture Quagmire: Navigating Office Politics and Hierarchies

The bureaucratic work environment is often characterized by its unique culture, which can include a complex hierarchy and a distinct brand of office politics. For individuals who navigate these spaces, the mastery of interpersonal dynamics becomes as critical as their professional skill set. It's not enough to merely do one's job competently; understanding and engaging with the multifaceted social fabric of the organization is essential for career advancement and effective governance.

Understanding the Undercurrents of Office Politics: Office politics can either serve as a conduit for success or become an obstacle. The reality is that perception, influence, and relationships drive decisions alongside policies and data. Recognizing the undercurrents of these politics can be as critical as mastering one's official duties. It involves not only being politically savvy but also having the ability to read between the lines of what is said and unsaid in meetings, emails, and casual conversations. It's about identifying allies, understanding opponents, and navigating the social dynamics with finesse and ethical consideration.

In a government office, Sarah, a policy advisor, quickly learned that data alone does not change minds. By building a coalition of interests and aligning her proposals with the priorities of key influencers, she could effectively translate her data into policy. Her success hinged on her ability to present her findings within the framework of what mattered to the decision-makers: the potential political wins, cost savings, or public approval that could result from adopting her recommendations.

For public servants like Sarah navigating these waters with integrity and strategic acumen is a critical skill. Her journey in the government office exemplifies this skillful navigation, demonstrating that effective policy advocacy often extends beyond factual data and into the realm of influencing and aligning with key decision-makers. This balance, when achieved with ethical grounding, can transform policy proposals from mere suggestions into impactful, implemented strategies. Through this delicate balance, public servants can not only foster positive change but also uphold the integrity and ideals of public service.

Hierarchy: The Visible and Invisible Ladders: Hierarchies in bureaucracies are not merely about ranks and titles but are also about the invisible networks of support and influence. Understanding who holds the 'real' power in an office can often lead to more strategic decisions and better outcomes.[20] It's not just the organizational chart that matters but the informal power structures that permeate the workspace — the trusted advisors, the gatekeepers, and the opinion leaders.[21]

Thomas, an administrative clerk, observed that the seemingly inconsequential role of scheduling for the senior executives positioned him uniquely as a nexus of information. With discretion and tact, he became an invaluable asset, and his insights into the organization's pulse were sought by those at higher ranks. His role gave him a vantage point, and by recognizing this, he was able to leverage his position to become a key player in the bureaucracy, demonstrating that power can come from unexpected places.

Thomas' experience in the bureaucratic hierarchy showcases a vital aspect of navigating public service institutions - the significance of recognizing and utilizing the informal networks of influence and information. His position as an administrative clerk, ostensibly low in the hierarchy, belied the strategic advantage it offered. By controlling the scheduling for senior executives, Thomas had a unique overview of the inner workings and priorities of the organization. His role, initially perceived as peripheral, placed him at the crossroads of vital communications and decisions.

This vantage point allowed Thomas to understand the nuances of power dynamics within the organization. He saw firsthand how decisions were made, who influenced them, and how various factors interplayed in the decision-making process. His discreet handling of this information, coupled with his ability to facilitate key meetings and interactions, gradually transformed his role. He became a subtle but critical cog in the organization's machinery.

Personal Values in a Predetermined Culture: Bureaucratic institutions are often perceived as rigid and resistant to change. However, they are made up of individuals, each with their own set of values. Balancing one's integrity while adapting to the institutional culture is a challenge many face. This balancing act requires a deft understanding of the nuances of the culture, identifying which aspects of one's personal values can be expressed and contribute to the organization's growth, and which may need to be tempered in service of the collective mission.

Emily, a communications specialist, found her creative approaches stifled by the agency's conservative culture. Instead of conceding, she sought common ground by demonstrating how her ideas could enhance the agency's mission within acceptable risk parameters. Her persistence paid off, slowly shifting the culture toward a more open-minded approach to communication strategies. By presenting her ideas with clear benefits to the organization, and framing them in a way that did not threaten the existing culture, Emily was able to enact change and stay true to her values.

Emily's journey within her agency highlights the intricate dance of aligning personal values with a pre-existing bureaucratic culture. Her story is a testament to the fact that bureaucratic systems, despite their rigidity, are not impervious to change initiated from within. Her success in integrating creative communication strategies into a traditionally conservative environment underscores the importance of strategic adaptation and perseverance.

This experience illustrates that while individuality may seem at odds with bureaucratic culture, there is room for personal values to influence and enrich the institutional landscape. Emily's approach of seeking common ground and aligning her innovative ideas with the agency's broader mission was key. She navigated the fine line between maintaining her creative integrity and respecting the established norms and values of the agency.

The Tempo of Change: The pace of change in a bureaucratic environment is notoriously slow. This can be frustrating to those accustomed to quicker decision-making processes, but it also ensures thoroughness and consideration. Navigating this tempo requires a recalibration of expectations and an appreciation for the processes that, while sometimes ponderous, are designed to prevent hasty decisions that could have far-reaching consequences.[22]

Mark, coming from a startup background, was initially exasperated with the slow-moving wheels of government. Over time, he learned to navigate this tempo, using the extra time for deeper research, building stronger cases for his projects, and engaging stakeholders more fully, which eventually led to meaningful reforms. Mark's journey was one of adaptation; he learned that within the constraints of the bureaucracy, there were opportunities for reflection and refinement that often led to superior outcomes.

Mark's transition from the fast-paced startup world to the methodical environment of bureaucracy serves as a powerful narrative on the value of adapting to different tempos of change. His initial frustration with the slow pace is a common sentiment among many who enter the public sector. However, his journey underscores the importance of patience and the strategic use of time in a bureaucratic setting.

Mark's evolution from exasperation to effective navigation within the system reveals a critical lesson: the slow pace of bureaucracy, often criticized, can be a boon for thoughtful deliberation and comprehensive planning. As he adjusted to this new rhythm, Mark discovered that the extended timelines allowed for more in-depth research, fostering a deeper understanding of the issues at hand. This additional time enabled him to build robust cases for his proposals, ensuring that when decisions were made, they were well-informed and substantively sound.

Moreover, Mark's experience highlights the significance of stakeholder engagement in bureaucratic processes. The slower pace provided him ample opportunities to consult with a wider array of stakeholders, ensuring diverse perspectives were considered. This thoroughness not only enhanced the quality of his projects but also built a broader base of support, facilitating smoother implementation and greater impact.

Negotiating the Terrain of Tradition: In bureaucracies, tradition often holds a significant weight. Innovators in these spaces must learn to negotiate with the established ways, finding opportunities to introduce new ideas without upending valued traditions. This delicate dance involves respect for the past while steadily pushing the boundaries toward progress, understanding that transformation in such environments is often evolutionary rather than revolutionary. [23]

Navigating the landscape of bureaucratic tradition is a tightrope between respect for established practices and the drive for innovation. This challenge is particularly poignant for those who enter these environments with a vision for change, only to find themselves confronted with the inertia of long-standing traditions and procedures. The key to success in this context lies in a nuanced approach that honors the past while gently ushering in the new.

For instance, consider the story of Laura, an IT specialist brought into a government agency to modernize its technology infrastructure. She quickly realized that her ambitious plans for digital transformation were meeting resistance, not due to a lack of merit, but because they clashed with deeply ingrained operational habits and norms. Laura's strategy was to introduce change incrementally. She started with small-scale projects that demonstrated the tangible benefits of modern technology, thereby gaining the trust and support of her colleagues. Gradually, as these smaller successes accumulated, they laid the groundwork for more significant changes.

Laura's approach exemplifies the art of balancing innovation with tradition. By implementing new ideas in a way that was non-threatening and clearly beneficial, she was able to build a coalition of support, even among the most tradition-bound members of her organization. Her respect for the existing culture, combined with her strategic, step-by-step method of introducing change, allowed her to transform the agency's technology landscape without alienating her peers.

This narrative underscores a fundamental truth about change in bureaucratic settings: it is most effective when it is evolutionary, not revolutionary. Change agents like Laura who recognize and work within the constraints of tradition, leveraging it as a foundation rather than viewing it as an obstacle, are often the ones who achieve lasting and meaningful progress. Their journey illustrates the power of patient, respectful negotiation with the terrain of tradition, proving that even in the most rigid environments, there is always room for thoughtful and well-executed innovation.

1.6 Navigating Bureaucracy with Emotional Baggage

Embarking on a journey through the bureaucratic labyrinths can often be a daunting venture, more so for those carrying the additional weight of personal trauma. The stoic hallways and the rigid structures of a challenging environment do not bend easily to accommodate the complex human stories that employees bring to their workplace every day. Yet, it is within these very structures that individuals must find a way to cultivate resilience and strive for excellence.

The ripple effects of personal trauma are wide-reaching, influencing an individual's behavior, professional relationships, and productivity. Trauma, in its essence, is a disruptor of normalcy; it alters one's baseline of operation, impacts decision-making processes, and can upend the delicate balance of professional dynamics. Within the confines of bureaucracy, where order and predictability are often prized, the unpredictable nature of trauma responses can seem like a misfit.[24]

Yet, there lies a paradox; the very predictability and structure of bureaucratic systems can, at times, offer a refuge for those seeking stability. For some, the routine tasks and clear expectations provide a framework within which they can begin to rebuild a sense of control and predictability in their lives. As someone who has witnessed colleagues navigating these waters, I've seen both the struggles and the quiet victories that often go unnoticed.

For instance, I recall a colleague, Robin, who had endured significant personal loss. Her work within our government agency became a sanctuary of sorts. The regularity of her duties allowed her to find a rhythm in her days that buffered the chaos she felt inside. Her story is a testament to the potential for professional environments to aid in the healing process, providing structure amid personal turmoil.

However, this is not a universal experience. For others, the red tape and the often impassive façade of bureaucracy can exacerbate the feelings of alienation and helplessness that are hallmarks of trauma. The challenge for organizations, then, is to become adept at recognizing and responding to these diverse needs, to transform into entities that not only allow for but actively support the healing journey of their employees.

It is crucial for organizations to implement a trauma-informed perspective—a lens through which the invisible burdens of employees are acknowledged and accommodated. This perspective considers the whole person, recognizing that personal experiences do not stay neatly outside the office doors but walk in with us each day and influence our interactions and work.

Creating a resilient workplace for trauma survivors involves more than just reactive measures; it requires a proactive and thoughtful approach. It might involve flexible scheduling or modifying the physical environment to reduce potential triggers. For example, providing a quiet space for breaks can be a simple yet effective strategy for someone who may get overwhelmed by sensory overload due to anxiety or post-traumatic stress.[25]

Professional development, too, must be handled with care and sensitivity. Trauma survivors may require different approaches to learning and mentorship. Tailored support systems can make a significant difference in their professional journey. Sarah, for instance, thrived under a mentor who provided her with gentle guidance and understood the value of flexible goal-setting.

Equally important is the need for accessible mental health resources, such as confidential counseling services or support groups. An initiative I helped develop at my workplace was the introduction of a peer support program, which paired employees with trained colleagues who could offer empathy and understanding in a less formal setting.

The integration of personal experiences, including trauma, into professional life, is not merely about creating a supportive work environment. It's about redefining organizational culture to recognize that our personal narratives shape us as professionals. They influence how we lead, collaborate, and innovate. For organizations, the insight and empathy derived from employees' diverse life experiences are invaluable assets that can drive authentic connection and creativity.

By fostering an environment that not only tolerates but embraces the full spectrum of employee experiences, organizations can become places where breakthroughs in bureaucracy are possible. In these spaces, resilience is not an individual struggle but a collective asset, and excellence is achieved not in spite of challenges but because of the strength garnered in overcoming them.

As we forge ahead in creating more resilient bureaucracies, it is important to remember the stories of people like Robin. It is in these personal journeys that we find the most potent lessons for transformation, both on an individual and organizational level. The commitment to this transformation is not just a matter of compassion but a strategic imperative for organizations aiming to thrive amid complexity and change.

The concept of "red tape" is not merely a metaphor but a tangible reality that can often lead to a sense of frustration and stagnation. It is the multitude of forms, the layers of approval, and the meticulous, sometimes seemingly redundant, procedures that are designed for fairness and accountability but can, in practice, stifle initiative and creativity.

The resilience to thrive in such environments is akin to that required by a mariner navigating treacherous waters—both must learn the currents, anticipate the storms, and utilize every tool at their disposal to reach their destination. Within bureaucracies, these tools include an understanding of the system's intricacies, the development of strategic relationships, and the cultivation of personal coping mechanisms that support one's mental and emotional health.

One key strategy is the development of a solid network within the organization. Building relationships across departments and levels can not only facilitate the flow of information but also provide support during challenging times. It's the friendly face in the procurement department who can guide a complex requisition through the process, or the seasoned colleague who can offer insight into the unspoken rules that govern the organizational culture.[26]

Another important resilience-building approach is the proactive management of one's workload.

This includes setting realistic deadlines, communicating effectively with supervisors and team members about capacity, and advocating for oneself when the weight of the workload threatens to overwhelm. For those with a history of trauma, self-care takes on an added layer of importance in the workplace. This can involve setting boundaries to ensure work does not encroach upon time for rest and recovery, engaging in regular physical activity to manage stress, and seeking out mental health support when needed.

Empowering oneself with knowledge is also critical. Understanding the legal frameworks, policies, and rationale behind bureaucratic procedures can transform perceptions of red tape from barriers to necessary steps in a larger process. It can also highlight opportunities for innovation within the bounds of the system.

One should not overlook the value of finding purpose and meaning within their role, even in a bureaucracy. Aligning one's work with personal values and goals can mitigate the sense of dissonance that may arise and foster a greater sense of personal fulfillment and professional accomplishment.

Leaders within bureaucracies have a role to play as well. By fostering an environment that values not only the end goals but also the well-being of the individuals who work towards them, they can create a culture of resilience. This can involve offering training and resources to help employees navigate the bureaucracy more effectively, recognizing and rewarding creativity and innovation, and promoting policies that prioritize mental health.[27]

Section Coaching:

Navigating bureaucracy with emotional baggage is akin to walking through a maze with a blindfold—it can feel disorienting, frustrating, and isolating. Yet, within the public sector's structured environment, there's a latent opportunity to channel our personal struggles into professional excellence and meaningful change. It demands a deliberate and empathetic approach to our daily interactions, our system navigation, and most importantly, our self-care.

Fostering Stability in Structure

For those grappling with personal trauma, the predictable nature of bureaucratic work can serve as a stabilizing force. The regularity of tasks and clear expectations can act as a steadying hand through the tumult of emotional upheaval. But this stability doesn't come passively; it's cultivated through active engagement with the work and its purpose.

Building Resilience in Routine

The daily grind, often laden with repetitive tasks, can be transformed into a meditative practice, a space where focus on the task at hand provides a respite from inner turmoil. It is in the mastery of these routines and the small victories in efficiency and service that one can find a sense of accomplishment and a building of resilience.

Creating Connections within the System

The bureaucratic network, though complex, holds potential for deep connections. Building relationships with colleagues offers a support system that can provide both professional guidance and personal comfort. These alliances become crucial in navigating the system, offering a collaborative approach to overcoming challenges.

Understanding the Impact of One's Work

To find meaning in bureaucracy, it's essential to understand the impact of one's work on the community. Whether it's issuing licenses or drafting policies, each task has a ripple effect, touching lives and shaping experiences. Recognizing and valuing this impact infuses work with purpose and transforms mundane tasks into components of a larger, noble mission.

Advocating for Personal and Organizational Healing

As public servants, advocating for a workplace that recognizes and supports healing from trauma is both a personal and professional responsibility. It involves pushing for policies that provide mental health resources, support flexible work arrangements, and create an organizational culture that values employee well-being.

Cultivating Emotional Intelligence

Developing emotional intelligence is key to managing the weight of personal trauma while navigating bureaucratic systems. It enhances self-awareness, aids in managing stress, and improves interactions with colleagues and the public, fostering a more empathetic and effective work environment.

Implementing a Trauma-Informed Approach

A trauma-informed approach to public service means recognizing that behind each form, policy, or procedure, there may be an employee carrying unseen emotional baggage. It's about creating and advocating for workplace practices that consider these factors, ensuring that the public sector is not only efficient but compassionate.

Pursuing Growth and Development

Professional growth and personal healing can go hand-in-hand. Seeking out mentorship, training, and development opportunities can provide a sense of progress and a distraction from personal struggles. Moreover, they can enhance one's ability to contribute to the organization's mission more meaningfully.

Maintaining Self-Care and Boundaries

In the midst of bureaucratic demands, self-care cannot be an afterthought. It's imperative to establish and maintain healthy boundaries between work and personal life. This includes taking regular breaks, engaging in activities that promote relaxation and mental health, and seeking support when needed.

Embracing the Journey

Navigating bureaucracy with emotional baggage is not a linear journey; it is fraught with setbacks and triumphs. Embracing this journey, with all its complexities, can lead to a richly rewarding career in public service, marked by personal growth and professional fulfillment.

By addressing these strategies, public servants can begin to see the bureaucracy not as a machine of impersonal processes but as a living organism that thrives on the well-being of its parts. In this realization lies the potential for personal healing, professional excellence, and ultimately, the transformation of public service into a force that is as humane as it is functional.

In the complex dance between maintaining high performance and managing the psychological impacts of trauma within a bureaucratic setting, there are no easy answers. However, there is a path forward that involves recognizing the unique challenges and strengths of each individual, cultivating a supportive network, and fostering an organizational culture that recognizes and addresses the multifaceted nature of employee well-being.

By implementing these strategies, both individuals and organizations can transform the bureaucratic labyrinth from a source of frustration into a journey of empowerment. The result is not only a more resilient workforce but also a more adaptive and responsive organization that can meet the challenges of a changing world.

CHAPTER 2

The Weight of Paperwork: Emotional Labor in Public Service

2.1. The Hidden Burdens of Bureaucratic Work

Public service is a call that resonates with the core values of many individuals; it is a pursuit steeped in the ideals of community, duty, and governance. This noble endeavor, often envisioned as a mechanism for societal structure and support, belies a less visible strain borne by its stewards. It's a strain not, in many cases, of physical exertion but of continuous emotional expenditure—a kind of labor not accounted for in budgets or balance sheets.[28] Beneath the poised exteriors of public servants lies an often-unacknowledged aspect of the job: the emotional labor inherent in bureaucratic work.[29] This chapter delves deeply into the concealed emotional burdens that public servants carry, their multifaceted impact, and the potential for transformation when these challenges are not only recognized but actively managed. By exploring the nuance of this labor and its pervasiveness, we can chart a course toward a more fulfilling and emotionally sustainable career in public service.

Understanding Emotional Labor: Emotional labor, a term coined by sociologist Arlie Hochschild, refers to the process by which workers manage their emotions to fulfill the emotional requirements of their job. In the realm of public service, the scope of this labor is vast, encompassing the empathetic handling of public inquiries, the management of interpersonal dynamics within teams, and the stoic composure in the face of bureaucratic inefficiencies. A survey by the American Psychological Association found that more than half of government employees experience high levels of stress due to the emotionally demanding nature of their work.[30] These findings shine a light on a pervasive issue that extends beyond individual encounters to the very fabric of the public sector, underscoring the profound need for strategies that address this often silent strain.[31]

The emotional demands on public servants are indeed multifaceted, affecting various aspects of their professional lives. At the forefront are the challenges posed by handling public inquiries. This aspect of their work often involves more than just providing information or solutions; it requires a deep sense of empathy. Public servants frequently encounter individuals who are distressed, frustrated, or confused. Managing these interactions necessitates an ability to not only understand and address the specific concerns raised but also to provide emotional support and reassurance. However, this must be balanced with maintaining professional boundaries, ensuring that the empathetic engagement does not compromise the objectivity and fairness expected in public service.

Internally, the dynamics within government entities can be complex and demanding. Public servants often work in teams, and these environments can be breeding grounds for varied opinions and perspectives. Managing these dynamics involves more than just technical skills; it requires emotional intelligence to balance differing views, navigate conflicts, and foster a cooperative atmosphere. The ability to understand and manage one's own emotions, as well as those of colleagues, is crucial in maintaining a positive and productive work environment. This internal emotional labor directly impacts team morale and efficiency. A team that is emotionally well-balanced and cohesive is more likely to be effective in delivering public services.

Bureaucratic inefficiencies add another layer to the emotional labor of public servants. These inefficiencies, characterized by red tape and procedural delays, can be frustrating not just for the public but also for those working within the system. Public servants must often navigate these inefficiencies while trying to provide the best possible service to the public. This requires a high level of emotional regulation to maintain composure and a positive outlook in the face of systemic challenges. It's about striking a balance between accepting certain realities of the bureaucratic system and continuously seeking ways to improve it. This balance is crucial in preventing burnout and maintaining a sense of purpose and motivation.

In essence, the emotional labor in public service is a juggling act that requires public servants to be empathetic and effective communicators with the public, while also being adept at managing internal team dynamics and systemic challenges. Recognizing and addressing these aspects of emotional labor is key to supporting the well-being of public servants and enhancing the overall quality and efficiency of public service.

The Weight of Empathy and Expectation: Empathy, the ability to understand and share the feelings of another, is the bedrock upon which public service is built. However, the expectation to remain perpetually empathetic, to consistently provide emotional support while performing one's duties, can lead to an insidious form of exhaustion.[32] The daily grind of paperwork, often perceived as a mere procedural necessity, is in reality a tapestry of human stories and needs, each interaction laden with emotional nuances. This emotional give-and-take is scarcely acknowledged in official job descriptions or performance evaluations, yet it is pivotal to the effectiveness and satisfaction of those who serve.

The weight of empathy in public service is substantial and multifaceted. Empathy, at its core, involves understanding and sharing the feelings of others, a critical aspect for those in public service roles. However, the expectation for public servants to remain perpetually empathetic presents unique challenges. Consistently providing emotional support while managing their professional responsibilities can lead to a form of exhaustion that is often overlooked. This emotional fatigue is not just about the physical demands of the job but also about the continuous emotional engagement required in their daily interactions.

In public service, each piece of paperwork, each policy implementation, and each public inquiry is more than just a task; it is an interaction that involves human stories and needs. Public servants routinely encounter individuals in distress or crisis, and each of these encounters requires not only a procedural response but also an emotional one. The ability to navigate these emotional nuances is a critical skill, yet this aspect of their work is rarely acknowledged in official job descriptions or performance evaluations. Despite its lack of formal recognition, empathy is pivotal to the effectiveness and satisfaction of public servants. It is what enables them to connect with the public in a meaningful way and to provide services that are not only efficient but also compassionate.

The tension between empathy and expectation in public service shapes the experiences of those in the field in profound ways. Public servants are often expected to maintain a high level of emotional engagement with the public while simultaneously managing their workload and adhering to bureaucratic procedures. This balancing act can be draining, as it requires constant adjustment between professional responsibilities and emotional responsiveness. The challenge lies in maintaining this balance without succumbing to burnout or becoming desensitized.

This tension also influences the delivery of services to the public. When public servants are emotionally overwhelmed or exhausted, their ability to provide high-quality services can be compromised. Conversely, when they are supported in managing their emotional labor, they are better equipped to engage with the public empathetically, leading to improved service delivery. Understanding and addressing the emotional demands of public service is therefore essential. It involves recognizing the emotional labor involved, providing support to manage this labor, and acknowledging the vital role empathy plays in the effective delivery of public services.

Navigating Emotional Complexity: For public servants, acknowledging the emotional dimensions of our work can serve as a catalyst for empowerment. It enables us to approach our duties with a sense of realism and self-awareness that buffers against burnout.[33] By adopting emotional intelligence as a skill set, we can revolutionize our

interactions with the machinery of bureaucracy and the public whom
we serve. The Emotional Intelligence Appraisal, developed by researchers
Travis Bradberry and Jean Greaves, provides a pragmatic framework for
understanding and improving emotional competencies, which can be
invaluable for public servants.[34]

Emotional intelligence (EI) plays a pivotal role in this context. It
refers to the ability to perceive, control, and evaluate emotions – both
one's own and those of others. For public servants, developing EI can lead
to more effective communication, enhanced problem-solving skills, and
better management of stress and conflict. In essence, EI can revolutionize
interactions within the bureaucratic machinery and improve the quality
of service delivered to the public.

Incorporating EI into the skill set of public servants can have
transformative effects. For instance, it can lead to more empathetic
policy making and implementation, where the needs and emotions of the
citizenry are carefully considered. It can also foster healthier workplace
dynamics, where conflicts are resolved constructively and the emotional
well-being of employees is prioritized.

Moreover, EI equips public servants to navigate the often challenging
and stressful landscape of public service more effectively. It helps
them understand and manage their own emotions, which is crucial
in high-pressure environments. It also enables them to recognize and
appropriately respond to the emotions of others, whether it's a colleague
or a member of the public.

The impact of emotional labor on the public sector is not just
theoretical but is substantiated by empirical data. Studies indicate
that emotional labor can have a profound impact on job satisfaction
and turnover rates. Findings from the Public Administration Review
demonstrate that employees who report high emotional labor also
report higher levels of exhaustion and burnout, suggesting a clear link
between emotional demands and workplace wellbeing. Paradoxically, the
emotional connection to the community and the sense of purpose derived
from helping others can be sources of great satisfaction, presenting a
complex dynamic between the costs and rewards of emotional labor.

This section presents a nuanced analysis of this data, underscoring the importance of emotional labor in shaping the landscape of public service.

2.2. Balancing Empathy and Efficiency

In the heart of public service lies the delicate dance between empathy and efficiency, two forces often seen at odds in the realm of bureaucracy. This balance requires not just skill but a profound understanding of the human aspect of governance. Empathy demands time and patience, enabling a more in-depth engagement with the needs and emotions of citizens, while efficiency calls for swift, decisive action—sometimes at the expense of personal touch. Striking this balance is not just an art; it is the lifeblood of effective public service, a harmonious blend that, when mastered, transforms the mechanical act of governance into an expression of collective stewardship and care.

The dichotomy between empathy and efficiency can be deceptive. In truth, they are not mutually exclusive but can, in fact, complement each other. Empathetic responses build a bridge of trust between the government and its citizens, setting the foundation for more effective and efficient future interactions. When citizens feel understood, they are more likely to engage constructively with public services. An efficient system that fails to incorporate empathy can inadvertently marginalize individuals, rendering services ineffective for those who may not fit the standard mold.

A study by the Journal of Organizational Behavior highlighted that organizations which focus on customer empathy outperform their counterparts by 2-to-1 in financial performance.[35] When we translate this to the public sector, it suggests that greater civic satisfaction, achieved through empathetic engagement, can lead to reduced service costs and an overall improved public perception of government institutions.[36] The true measure of a system's efficiency lies not in the rapidity of its processes but in its precision and responsiveness to the nuanced needs it serves. Here, empathy transforms from a soft skill to a strategic asset, offering a beacon for systemic transformation and operational excellence.

But how do we infuse sprawling bureaucracies with a spirit of empathy without compromising on end goals? It begins at the individual level. The strategy is two-pronged: nurturing personal competencies in emotional intelligence and cultivating institutional cultures that prioritize and reward empathetic service.[37] Organizations must create pathways for individual growth in empathy that resonate through the bureaucracy, ultimately influencing policy and procedure.

Achieving this balance necessitates a shift in the paradigm of efficiency. Efficiency in the public sector should be recalibrated, not measured solely by the number of cases closed or services delivered in a time frame but by the meaningful impact those services have on the community.[38] We must continually assess whether our actions are addressing the correct issues and improving the lives of the people we serve. The goal is to enhance traditional efficiency, augmenting it with empathetic efficacy—a holistic approach to serving the public good.

Real-world examples provide a blueprint for success. Take the Department of Motor Vehicles (DMV) in various states, which has taken strides to integrate customer feedback into process improvements. By listening to and valuing the public's input, these agencies have not only improved the quality of their services but have also witnessed significant gains in efficiency—shorter wait times and higher customer satisfaction rates are testament to the power of an empathetically driven approach.

However, the implementation of empathetic practices comes with its set of challenges. It demands investment in time, training, and a willingness to deviate from strict adherence to the rule book when human-centered discretion is warranted. Here lies the test of emotional resilience for public servants, a test that calls for courage and unwavering dedication to the core values of public service. The journey toward empathy-infused governance is complex and demanding, yet it is one that public servants must undertake if they are to fully honor their commitment to serving the public.

As we forge ahead, it is imperative to see empathy and efficiency not as foes but as partners in the quest to serve the public better. This partnership redefines the essence of public service, morphing it into a pursuit that not only fulfills the logistical demands of governance but also addresses the emotional and societal needs of the community. For public servants, the quest to balance these forces is our challenge, our mandate, and, ultimately, our distinct honor. This balance is not an endpoint but a continuous journey towards a more humane and effective public service—one that values each citizen and strives to reflect that in every policy, program, and interaction.

Section Coaching: Checklist for Balancing Empathy and Efficiency in Public Service

Understand the Interplay: Recognize that empathy and efficiency are not mutually exclusive but complementary in public service. Acknowledge the importance of both in serving the public effectively.

Build Empathetic Relationships: Develop strategies to connect with citizens on a personal level. Encourage staff to take the time to understand the needs and emotions of the public they serve.

Integrate Emotional Intelligence: Foster emotional intelligence within the organization. Offer training and resources to help staff develop skills like active listening, empathy, and emotional regulation.

Prioritize Responsive Service: Shift the focus from mere speed and quantity of service delivery to the quality and responsiveness of services. Ensure that actions are addressing the correct issues and positively impacting the community.

Encourage Constructive Feedback: Create channels for staff and public feedback. Use insights gained to improve services and address any shortcomings in both empathy and efficiency.

Promote a Culture of Empathy: Cultivate a workplace culture that values and rewards empathetic engagement with colleagues and the public. Recognize and celebrate instances where staff demonstrate exceptional empathy.

Balance Individual Needs with Systemic Goals: Find a balance between personal interactions and systemic efficiency. Ensure that individual staff members are empowered to make empathetic decisions while adhering to overall organizational goals.

Implement Strategic Asset Empathy: View empathy as a strategic asset, not just a soft skill. Apply it in policy-making and service delivery to enhance the relevance and impact of government actions.

Incorporate Public Input in Policy Making: Actively seek and value public input in the development and refinement of policies and procedures. Use this input to make services more inclusive and effective.

Enhance Traditional Efficiency Metrics: Redefine efficiency metrics to include the impact of services on the community. Focus on meaningful outcomes rather than just procedural outputs.

Learn from Real-World Examples: Study and learn from successful cases where empathy and efficiency have been balanced effectively, such as improvements in DMV processes.

Prepare for Challenges: Be prepared to invest time and resources in training and development. Encourage staff to embrace challenges as opportunities for growth and learning.

Regularly Evaluate and Adapt: Continuously assess the balance between empathy and efficiency, making adjustments as needed. Stay flexible and open to change based on feedback and evolving public needs.

Communicate the Vision: Clearly communicate the importance of balancing empathy and efficiency to all levels of the organization. Ensure that this balance is a key part of the public service ethos.

Sustain the Journey: Recognize that balancing empathy and efficiency is a continuous journey. Commit to long-term efforts in cultivating a more humane and effective public service.

2.3. From Stress to Success: Coping Mechanisms for Bureaucrats

Navigating the labyrinthine pathways of public service, bureaucrats often find themselves in the grips of stress that is both unique to the profession and, unfortunately, widely misunderstood. It is a kind of stress that does not recede when the office lights dim, nor does it respect the boundaries between personal and professional life. The chronic nature of bureaucratic stress, with its intricate tapestry woven from the threads of high stakes, public scrutiny, and red tape, can lead to an insidious and profound sense of burnout. But this stress need not be an endpoint. Instead, it can be a transformative force, a call to action for personal growth and systemic reform. Within this crucible of pressure, there exists the potential for immense personal transformation and professional evolution. This transformative force can compel bureaucrats to seek innovative solutions, embrace adaptability, and champion the kind of systemic reform that does not merely alter the surface of procedures but fundamentally reshapes the landscape of public service for the better.[39]

The coping mechanisms for bureaucrats must be as multifaceted as the stressors they encounter. Empirical studies underscore the value of individualized coping strategies; a meta-analysis found that tailored approaches to stress management are notably more effective than generic programs.[40] Therefore, it is vital to craft a personalized toolkit of strategies that can turn the tide from stress to success.[41] These strategies might include a blend of cognitive-behavioral techniques to reframe negative thought patterns, emotional intelligence training to better navigate interpersonal dynamics, and time management methodologies to bring a sense of order to the often chaotic bureaucratic environment. Each bureaucrat must become an architect of their own wellbeing, constructing a fortress of habits and attitudes that protect and sustain them through the storms of public service.

One such tool is the cultivation of resilience, an attribute that has garnered significant attention in psychological research. The American Psychological Association delineates resilience as "the process of adapting well in the face of adversity, trauma, tragedy, threats, or significant sources of stress."[42] This adaptability can be nurtured through deliberate practice. Resilience-building activities may include mindfulness meditation to reduce emotional exhaustion, or engaging in regular physical exercise, which a vast array of research correlates with lowered stress levels. Building resilience is akin to strengthening a muscle; it requires consistent effort and a commitment to pushing beyond one's comfort zone. It might involve setting and overcoming small, incremental challenges, thus providing bureaucrats with a sense of accomplishment and mastery over their circumstances.[43]

Another powerful coping mechanism is the fostering of social support networks within the workplace. The Harvard Business Review highlights the correlation between strong workplace relationships and lower stress levels. Colleagues who understand the unique pressures of the bureaucratic environment can provide empathetic support, practical advice, and sometimes, a necessary sounding board for frustrations.[44] Moreover, these relationships can transcend the confines of the workplace, offering a sense of community and belonging that combats the isolation that stress can often breed. Cultivating these networks may require intentional outreach and vulnerability, creating spaces where honest conversations about the realities of bureaucratic work can occur without fear of repercussion or misunderstanding.

Skill development presents another avenue for mitigating stress. Pursuing continued education and professional development can empower bureaucrats with a greater sense of control over their work. This could range from honing technical skills to learning new bureaucratic navigation strategies, thereby enhancing a sense of competence and autonomy. Additionally, skill development can provide a diversion from daily stressors, offering an intellectual challenge that can rejuvenate a tired mind and invigorate a weary spirit. It can serve as a reminder that growth and learning are always possible, even in the most rigid of bureaucratic systems.

Moreover, the integration of creative problem-solving approaches can reframe obstacles as opportunities. Encouraging bureaucrats to engage in lateral thinking, to not just work within the system but to think outside its constraints, can spark innovation that both alleviates stress and leads to more effective governance. The potential of creative thinking to improve job satisfaction and performance in complex work environments is documented. Creative problem-solving encourages a sense of play and experimentation, a welcome reprieve from the often-serious nature of bureaucratic work, and it has the added benefit of potentially discovering unorthodox solutions to entrenched systemic issues.[45]

Journaling serves as both a reflective and proactive practice. Documenting the daily challenges and victories provides a valuable perspective on the trajectory of one's career and personal growth, and it serves as a reminder of the impact one's work has on the broader community. This practice aligns with research which indicates that expressive writing can alleviate stress and promote psychological well-being. [46] Journaling can be a private haven, a place for bureaucrats to process their experiences without judgment, to celebrate their successes, and to formulate plans for overcoming their challenges. It is a practice that honors the narrative of each individual, weaving their personal story into the grander narrative of public service.

A critical component of these coping mechanisms is the encouragement of a work culture that values and actively supports mental health. A study in the Journal of Organizational Behavior linked organizational culture with employee mental health outcomes, emphasizing the need for leadership to prioritize the psychological safety of their staff.[47] When the culture of an organization places a premium on mental health, it gives permission for its members to take the necessary steps to care for themselves. This cultural shift might involve introducing policies that promote work-life balance, creating clear channels for reporting and addressing workplace stress, and providing resources for mental health support, including access to counseling and stress management programs.

In transforming stress into success, bureaucrats must become students of their own experiences. They should observe, analyze, and adapt to their emotional and psychological responses, treating them as data points to guide their coping strategies. This introspective process not only benefits the individual but also becomes a conduit for broader systemic change, as the health of each bureaucrat reflects the health of the institution they serve. It is a journey of self-discovery that has far-reaching implications, shaping not only the individual but also the culture and efficacy of the bureaucracy itself. By acknowledging and attending to their own needs, bureaucrats can set a precedent for compassionate, mindful leadership that values the human element within the machinery of government.

Coping mechanisms, therefore, are not mere tools for survival; they are stepping stones to thriving in a complex system. They represent an ongoing commitment to personal development and an investment in the collective well-being of the institution of public service. As bureaucrats harness these strategies, they pave the way for a more resilient, responsive, and humane bureaucracy—a testament to the enduring spirit of those who choose to serve. This journey towards resilience and wellbeing is not a solitary one; it is a collective endeavor that enhances the capacity of public institutions to serve their communities with greater empathy, efficiency, and effectiveness. It is a path that leads from the individual to the institutional, from stress to success, and from a culture of endurance to one of flourishing.

Section Coaching:

The burden of this stress is not only the high-stakes decisions and public scrutiny but also the daily navigation of the processes that define bureaucracy. To pivot from stress to success, bureaucrats must equip themselves with a tailored set of coping mechanisms, crafted to withstand the pressures unique to the public sector and to catalyze personal and professional advancement.

Cognitive Reframing Techniques

One of the first tools in this personalized toolkit is cognitive reframing. By challenging negative thought patterns and reshaping them into a positive or proactive outlook, bureaucrats can transform perceived obstacles into challenges that invigorate rather than drain. This technique enables them to view bureaucratic hurdles not as personal affronts or insurmountable barriers but as opportunities for problem-solving and innovation.

Emotional Intelligence and Interpersonal Skills

Further, developing emotional intelligence is crucial for navigating the emotional landscape of public service. Cultivating an ability to recognize one's emotions, understand the emotional context of colleagues and constituents, and navigate interpersonal relationships with empathy can reduce the personal toll of bureaucratic stress. It enables bureaucrats to forge supportive relationships and engage in constructive conflict resolution, thereby creating a more harmonious work environment.

Efficient Time Management

Time management is another cornerstone of coping in bureaucracy. By prioritizing tasks, setting realistic goals, and communicating effectively with colleagues and superiors about workload and capacity, bureaucrats can alleviate the overwhelm that often accompanies a high-volume workload. Moreover, efficient time management allows for better work-life balance, which is essential for long-term career sustainability and personal well-being.

Resilience through Mindfulness and Physical Wellness

To build resilience, bureaucrats can practice mindfulness meditation to anchor themselves in the present moment and mitigate emotional exhaustion. Coupled with regular physical activity—proven to reduce stress and enhance mood—these practices foster a sense of control and self-efficacy. They are the bedrock upon which bureaucrats can maintain their health and energy, ensuring they have the capacity to tackle the demands of their roles.

Cultivation of Supportive Networks

The power of community cannot be overstated. Cultivating a network of colleagues who can relate to the unique challenges of bureaucratic work provides not just a safety net but also a source of collective wisdom. These networks serve as a platform for sharing strategies, offering encouragement, and fostering a sense of camaraderie and collective purpose.

Professional Development and Continuous Learning

Continual professional development is a proactive strategy to combat stress. By enhancing skills and competencies, bureaucrats can increase their confidence and sense of agency within the system. This growth mindset not only prepares them to handle current challenges but also positions them to anticipate and adapt to future changes within the bureaucratic landscape.

Creativity within Constraints

Moreover, embracing creative problem-solving within the constraints of bureaucracy can lead to significant job satisfaction and innovation. By thinking laterally and seeking novel solutions within the bounds of existing regulations, bureaucrats can circumvent frustration and find fulfillment in their ability to effect meaningful change.

Reflective Practices like Journaling

Journaling offers a reflective space for bureaucrats to process their daily experiences, track their professional growth, and remind themselves of their contributions to the public good. This practice of putting pen to paper can offer perspective, release tension, and reinforce personal and professional goals.

Advocacy for Mental Health

Advocating for a workplace culture that prioritizes mental health is essential. When organizations recognize the importance of mental well-being and provide resources and support, it can dramatically alter the landscape of public service, creating environments where bureaucrats can thrive rather than merely survive.

In transforming stress into success, bureaucrats must become architects of their own well-being, building a robust foundation that supports them through the trials of public service. These coping mechanisms form a comprehensive approach that not only mitigates the immediate effects of stress but also fosters a culture of resilience, adaptability, and continuous improvement. Through personalized coping strategies, bureaucrats can navigate the complexities of their roles with agility and emerge as champions of both personal well-being and public service excellence.

CHAPTER 3

Breaking the Chains: Overcoming Bureaucratic Trauma

3.1 Recognizing the Signs of Organizational Trauma

In the heart of every bureaucratic institution, beneath the veneer of structure and stability, lies the potential for organizational trauma. This trauma is not a singular event, but a pervasive and corrosive atmosphere that, if left unchecked, can permeate the very fabric of public service.[48] The landscape of government work, often seen as a bastion of continuity, hides beneath it the tremors of strain that can lead to systemic dysfunction. To confront and overcome it, we must first learn to recognize its signs, understanding that only through awareness can we initiate healing and change. Recognizing the signs of organizational trauma is akin to a diagnostic process in medicine—the first, critical step to recovery. It involves a careful and often uncomfortable examination of the norms and practices that define an organization's day-to-day reality.

Organizational trauma manifests in various forms, each symptomatic of a deeper malaise within the system. It is characterized by an atmosphere where individuals feel perpetually overwhelmed, unsupported, and entrapped in a cycle of negativity. These feelings of powerlessness and despair are the human response to a workplace environment that demands much yet offers little by way of personal fulfillment or collective purpose. A study by Strategic HR Review revealed that employees in high-stress environments, including public service sectors, reported feeling emotionally drained and detached from their work, indicative of a traumatic organizational culture.[49] This detachment is not merely a lack of job satisfaction; it is a sign of a deeper existential malaise that if left unaddressed, can erode the very foundations of effective governance.

One of the most salient indicators of such trauma is the pervasive sense of fear and anxiety that stifles innovation and risk-taking. Employees in traumatic bureaucratic environments often experience a fear of retribution for stepping outside of established norms. This fear creates invisible barriers to creativity and growth, as individuals learn to prioritize self-preservation over collaborative achievement. This culture of fear can lead to what researchers identify as moral injury, where individuals perpetually confront ethical dilemmas that conflict with their values, leading to profound psychological distress. Such injury can stagnate one's sense of professional integrity and diminish trust in the system, leading to a workforce that is disengaged and disillusioned.[50]

Additionally, high rates of absenteeism and employee turnover can be a distressing signal of a traumatized workplace. It's a red flag, often indicative of an environment where the day-to-day experience is so at odds with one's well-being that disengagement becomes a form of self-protection. When researchers examine sectors with high turnover rates, it often finds underlying issues of systemic dissatisfaction and unaddressed stressors that push individuals to seek relief outside the confines of their current roles.[51] Such data not only reflect the cost to the individual's quality of life but also underscore the inefficiency and lack of sustainability within the traumatized system.[52]

Communication breakdowns are another symptom, where the flow of information is disrupted by silos and gatekeeping. These are not just operational inefficiencies; they represent a deeper relational crisis where mistrust has become institutionalized. Studies find that in organizations with traumatic cultures, there is a significant correlation between poor communication and employee dissatisfaction. In such settings, information becomes a currency of power rather than a shared resource, which can create a hostile environment that hampers collaboration and trust. This is antithetical to the ethos of public service, which relies on transparent and open communication to serve the collective good.

Moreover, in such organizations, there is a noticeable decline in employee engagement and morale. The Gallup State of the Global Workplace report consistently highlights engagement as a key driver of productivity and satisfaction. However, in traumatic bureaucratic environments, employees often feel that their contributions are undervalued, leading to a decrease in initiative and a sense of helplessness. This disengagement is not a personal failure but a systemic issue that reflects a misalignment between an organization's stated values and its lived reality.

The presence of chronic fatigue and health complaints among employees can also point towards organizational trauma. Chronic stress is not merely a personal health issue; it is a public health concern that speaks volumes about the work environment. The European Agency for Safety and Health at Work has linked stressful work environments to physical health problems, indicating that sustained stressors within the workplace contribute to a host of health issues, ranging from hypertension to mental health disorders. These health issues are a clarion call for a change in the way we view and manage work within public service institutions.[53]

But recognizing these signs is not an exercise in futility; it is the first step towards creating a more resilient and healthy organization. By identifying these symptoms, we acknowledge the pervasive nature of the problem and begin the crucial work of diagnosing and addressing the underlying causes of bureaucratic trauma. It's an invitation to embark on a transformative journey that questions and reshapes the organizational norms that have led to the current state of affairs.

To move forward, we must shift our perspective and see these signs not as failings but as opportunities for profound transformation. When we acknowledge the stress and fear pervading our institutions, we challenge the status quo and begin to dismantle the harmful patterns that sustain them. This is an act of collective courage—a conscious choice to steer the ship away from turbulent waters towards a more nurturing and productive environment. Through this recognition, we open the door to a future where the well-being of public servants is not an afterthought, but a cornerstone of public service excellence. This future is not an unreachable utopia but a practical vision that can be achieved with sustained effort and commitment.

Addressing organizational trauma requires us to not only innovate but to fundamentally rethink the structures and policies that underpin our institutions. It demands an audacious reimagination of what it means to work within the public sector. It calls for leadership that is courageous and compassionate, capable of nurturing an environment where transparency, support, and genuine care for the well-being of each individual are the norm, not the exception. Such leadership doesn't just direct; it inspires and empowers, creating a space where employees can thrive and find meaning in their work.

The task is substantial, yet the path is illuminated by the knowledge that through confronting and healing from organizational trauma, we can forge a stronger, more empathetic, and effective public service. This path is not easy; it is fraught with challenges and resistance. Yet, it is a journey worth embarking on, with the promise of a workplace that not only functions efficiently but also honors the dignity and potential of every public servant. Let us, therefore, embark on this journey with the understanding that the recognition of trauma is the first step on the path to renewal. It is a path that leads us not only to heal the organization but also to rediscover the noble purpose at the heart of public service.

Section Coaching: Checklist for Recognizing the Signs of Bureaucratic Organizational Trauma

Assess Emotional Climate: Regularly gauge the emotional state of the workforce. Look for widespread feelings of helplessness, chronic fatigue, or a general atmosphere of despair.

Monitor Work-Life Balance: Be alert to changes in work-life balance among employees. An increase in late hours, working through weekends, or reduced vacation usage can be signs of organizational overstrain.

Evaluate Turnover Rates: Keep track of turnover rates. High turnover can indicate systemic issues, including burnout or dissatisfaction.

Track Absenteeism: Monitor absenteeism patterns. Frequent short-term absences can be a cry for help from overburdened employees.

Observe Communication Patterns: Watch for breakdowns in communication. Silos, information hoarding, or a lack of collaboration indicate a breakdown in organizational health.

Listen for Silence: Pay attention to what is not being said. A lack of upward feedback or silence in meetings can signal fear or disengagement.

Check for Ethical Strain: Be vigilant about signs of moral injury. Look for situations where employees are forced to act against their values.

Survey Employee Engagement: Conduct regular surveys to measure employee engagement and satisfaction. Sharp declines are often a precursor to deeper issues.

Identify Signs of Mistrust: Notice if there's a lack of trust in leadership or between departments. Mistrust can cripple an organization's ability to function effectively.

Watch for Innovation Stagnation: Keep an eye on the rate of innovation. A lack of new ideas or fear of suggesting them can be a result of an oppressive atmosphere.

Assess Decision-Making Efficacy: Examine the decision-making process. Delays and avoidance in decision-making can be a symptom of a traumatized organization.

Spot Stress-Related Health Issues: Look for an increase in stress-related health complaints among employees. Chronic stress can lead to both physical and mental health problems.

Review Resource Allocation: Ensure resources are being used effectively. Misallocation can lead to unnecessary stress and strain on employees.

Acknowledge and Address: When signs are identified, openly acknowledge them and take action. Denial can exacerbate the trauma.

Seek External Help: Consider engaging with external consultants or mental health professionals to evaluate the organization and suggest improvements.

Foster Open Dialogue: Create safe spaces for employees to express their concerns and experiences. Open dialogue can be the first step in healing.

Implement Support Structures: Build robust support structures for employees, including access to counseling and mental health services.

Lead by Example: Leadership must demonstrate a commitment to addressing and healing organizational trauma through transparent and authentic action.

Promote a Culture of Care: Work towards a culture that values each individual and their wellbeing, which in turn can mitigate the impacts of trauma.

Evaluate and Iterate: Regularly review the effectiveness of implemented strategies and be prepared to adapt and iterate based on feedback and results.

3.2. Healing from Within: Personal Stories of Overcoming Bureaucratic Trauma

The journey of healing from bureaucratic trauma often begins in quiet, personal revolutions within the hearts of those it affects. This intricate process unfolds in the intimate corners of the mind, where resilience is forged in the face of adversity. It is within these stories of individual struggle, perseverance, and triumph that we find the most potent lessons for institutional transformation. This section aims to delve into the personal narratives that not only inspire but also illuminate the path to healing and growth within the complex labyrinth of government bureaucracy. These stories resonate deeply, offering not just solace but a guiding light for others engulfed in similar battles, demonstrating that change, although daunting, is within reach.

Mandy, a dedicated public servant within the Department of Health, who found herself battling the waves of burnout and disillusionment. Her tale is a testament to the human spirit's resilience, a beacon for those adrift in the sea of bureaucratic malaise. Mandy recalls the moment she realized that her work environment was not merely challenging but toxic—a quagmire of apathy and despondence. Absenteeism was high, morale was low, and her colleagues were suffering in silence, trapped in the inertia of a dysfunctional system. Through her story, we learn the importance of mindfulness and self-advocacy in the workplace.

Mandy's transformation began with small, yet pivotal, steps. She started organizing informal support groups during lunch hours, which created a ripple effect, fostering a sense of community and collective care. This act of solidarity and leadership sparked a shift in the office dynamics, leading to a tangible decrease in absenteeism by 15% within her division, according to an internal report. Mandy's story is not unique; it echoes the experiences of many who find healing by turning towards one another for support—proof that within the frameworks that confine us, there are still opportunities for connection and growth.

Then there's Michael, a case worker from a social service agency, who struggled under the weight of bureaucratic inefficiencies that hampered his ability to serve those in need effectively. He was mired in a system that seemed to work against the very people it was designed to assist. His breakthrough came not through sweeping policy changes, but when he chose to focus on what he could control—his own approach to the work. By adopting Agile methodologies, often used in software development, and adapting them to his work context, he not only revolutionized his own productivity but also injected a dose of much-needed enthusiasm into his team. He improved his case processing time by 30%, a significant metric that highlights the potential for transformation even within the most rigid of structures. Michael's story teaches us that sometimes, the tools for healing and improvement lie in the cross-pollination of ideas from seemingly unrelated fields, signaling that innovation often thrives at the intersection of diverse concepts and practices.

Amidst the narratives of change, one cannot overlook the compelling story of Aisha, a procurement officer in a large city government, who faced the stark reality of systemic discrimination. The journey of healing for Aisha was less about personal resilience and more about systemic confrontation. It began with her decision to confront these issues head-on by pursuing advanced training in diversity and inclusion. She didn't stop at just equipping herself with knowledge; she became a vanguard for change within her department. Aisha used her newfound knowledge to advocate for policy changes that led to a 20% increase in minority-owned business contracts within two years. Her story is a powerful reminder of the courage needed to address and rectify systemic issues from within.

Aisha's narrative underscores the critical need for policies that not only acknowledge diversity but actively promote inclusion. Her determination and her willingness to initiate difficult conversations paved the way for more equitable practices within her city government. Her triumph over institutional inertia and her victories in the name of equality resonate with a potent message: the individual's healing journey can catalyze far-reaching organizational and societal transformation.

These stories bring forth key strategies for healing from bureaucratic trauma, each a puzzle piece in the vast mosaic of change: Establishing peer support systems that provide a safe space for sharing and mutual aid, as exemplified by Sarah's lunchtime gatherings, becomes a bedrock for collective healing. Embracing innovative approaches and methodologies to improve efficiency and satisfaction, as Michael's adaptation of Agile principles illustrates, encourages a shift in perspective and practice. Advocating for inclusivity and equity, and using personal influence to effect policy change, is embodied in Aisha's fight for diversity and her impact on procurement policies. Research underscores the value of these strategies. A survey conducted by the Center for American Progress found that when employees engage in peer support programs, there is a reported increase in job satisfaction and a decrease in turnover intentions by as much as 24%.[54] Furthermore, innovation in processes is not just about efficiency; a Harvard Business Review study showed that employees who are encouraged to innovate report higher job satisfaction and performance.[55]

The path of healing is often long and winding, marked by small victories and significant milestones alike. It requires a blend of personal fortitude and systemic awareness. As these personal stories reveal, healing from bureaucratic trauma is not a solitary endeavor but a collective journey. It demands that we look within to find the strength to enact change without. It challenges us to adopt a new lens through which to view our professional landscapes—one that is rooted in empathy, fosters creative problem-solving, and champions progressive change.

As we immerse ourselves in these narratives, we discover not just the power of the human spirit but also practical strategies that can be applied across the spectrum of public service. These are stories that do not just belong to the individuals who lived them; they are blueprints for a more compassionate, efficient, and resilient public sector. They represent the silent battles and the unsung heroes who dare to transform a moment of struggle into a movement for change.

The significance of these stories extends beyond the individuals; they are catalysts for broader institutional change. They challenge us to look beyond the constraints of our roles and the limits of our systems. By embracing vulnerability, fostering innovation, and advocating for justice and equity, we can begin to heal from within. The data, the stories, and the lessons they impart are clear: change is possible, and it begins with the courage of those who dare to make a difference, one personal revolution at a time.

3.3 Transforming Pain into Policy: When Personal Struggle Drives Change

In the heart of every policy, there is a pulse—a human story driving its inception, development, and implementation. The narrative of change within bureaucratic structures often finds its origins not in data points or policy papers, but in the lived experiences of those it affects.

Pain has a voice, and in the context of bureaucracy, it often goes unheard amidst the hum of everyday functioning. Yet, for those who endure it, the pain of systemic inefficiencies, the ache of unrecognized labor, and the sting of institutional indifference can become catalysts for transformation. Personal struggles are not merely obstacles; they can be the very tools that chisel away at the monolith of bureaucracy to reveal a more responsive and empathetic framework for governance.[56]

Consider the story of Maria, a social worker who grappled with the limitations of her agency's outdated filing system which delayed service delivery to vulnerable clients. The frustration and helplessness she experienced turned into a quest for a solution that eventually led her to advocate for digital transformation within her department. Drawing from her personal struggle, Maria's case prompted the development of an integrated case management system that reduced processing times by 40%, as indicated by a departmental efficiency review.

Maria's story exemplifies how personal challenges can foster policy innovations. According to a study by the Digital Government Society, when agencies adopt technology inspired by front-line employee input, there is a 60% improvement in client satisfaction scores.[57] This demonstrates the tangible impact of employee-driven innovation on the efficacy of public services.

The transformation of personal pain into policy is not a simple process. It requires a strategic approach to leverage one's experience to effect systemic change. It involves four critical steps: recognizing the pain points, envisioning a better system, harnessing personal experiences as a case for change, and advocating for this change through the appropriate channels.

Recognition is the first step. It's about understanding that the frustration one feels is a signal of a deeper, systemic issue. For example, James, an administrator bogged down by a procurement process steeped in redundancies, recognized that his frustration reflected a larger problem affecting departmental performance. The second step is envisioning a better system. James imagined a procurement process that was streamlined and transparent, saving time and reducing confusion for staff. His vision was backed by evidence from a Government Accountability Office report, which stated that streamlining procurement processes could reduce administrative costs by up to 20%.

Harnessing personal experiences as a case for change is the third step. James collected narratives from various colleagues, outlining the time and opportunities lost to cumbersome processes. This collection of experiences formed a compelling argument for change. Advocating through the right channels requires tactful navigation of the bureaucracy itself. James compiled his findings into a proposal and sought allies within the organization, gradually building a coalition that reached the decision-makers. Personal struggle becomes a beacon, guiding the development of policies that are not just theoretically sound but are tested and demanded by the reality of daily work in the public sector. Such policies are not only more likely to be effective, but also carry with them a sense of legitimacy and urgency that purely top-down initiatives often lack.

The conversion of hardship into policy is not merely theoretical. In the realm of healthcare, for instance, we find numerous policies that were born from the trials and tribulations of patients, families, and healthcare workers. The Mental Health Parity Act in the United States is one such policy that was significantly influenced by personal stories of inequality in treatment between physical and mental health conditions. This legislation, which faced initial resistance, gained momentum as more individuals shared their struggles with accessing mental health care, highlighting the human cost of inaction.

In the crafting of public policy, data is indispensable. However, equally important are the stories behind the data. According to a policy analysis by the Aspen Institute, initiatives that are rooted in personal narratives of affected individuals see a 35% higher rate of successful implementation. Data indeed provides the skeleton upon which policies are built, but it is the marrow of human experience that gives them life and purpose. Research published in the Policy Studies Journal suggests that policies informed by personal narratives have a higher likelihood of being embraced by those they aim to help, leading to better compliance and fewer implementation issues.[58]

Embracing the narrative of pain in policy-making also necessitates a cultural shift within bureaucratic institutions. It calls for a move away from a detached, impersonal approach to one that values empathy and understanding. It requires building a system where the voices of those on the front lines are amplified and where their experiences shape the foundations of policy. In training programs for public servants, incorporating modules that focus on narrative competence—the ability to listen to and interpret stories—can empower individuals to convert their experiences into advocacy for systemic change. These skills not only aid in policy development but also enhance communication with the public, thereby fostering trust and rapport.[59] Moreover, the digital era presents unprecedented opportunities to collect and disseminate personal stories widely, thus amplifying their impact on policy. Social media campaigns, for instance, can bring attention to specific bureaucratic challenges and galvanize public support for change, as seen with campaigns around climate change and public health issues.

The narrative of personal struggle also presents an opportunity for collaborative policy-making. By involving those affected in the policy development process, public institutions can create a more democratic, inclusive, and responsive governance model. This approach is evidenced by participatory budgeting practices, which have been shown to increase public engagement and satisfaction with governmental decisions.

In essence, the journey from personal pain to policy is about harnessing adversity for the greater good. It's about turning individual hardship into collective progress, and in doing so, demonstrating the incredible potential of human resilience and ingenuity. It's a process that not only produces more humane policies but also imbues the policymakers themselves with a deeper sense of purpose and connection to the communities they serve.

The challenge for us, then, is to listen—to truly hear the stories of those within our systems who are struggling, to validate their experiences, and to allow those narratives to guide our actions and reforms. It is only by doing so that we can ensure our policies are not just well-intentioned, but truly effective and grounded in the reality of human experience.

Maria's frustration with the filing system and James's struggle with the procurement process are more than isolated incidents; they represent a collective call for change. These individual stories of bureaucratic challenges and personal perseverance can be seen as threads in a larger tapestry of systemic transformation. When woven together, they form a picture of what our public institutions could become: efficient, empathetic, and inclusive.

Policy changes driven by personal narratives can also shift public perception, illustrating that government can be a force for positive change, responsive to the needs and well-being of its citizens. This can rekindle trust in public institutions, which is crucial in a time when skepticism and disillusionment are all too common. By grounding policy in the realities of human experience, by listening to and learning from the struggles of those we serve, we can break the chains of bureaucratic trauma and pave the way for a government that not only serves its people but also elevates and empowers them. In this new paradigm, each personal struggle is not an endpoint but a beginning—a spark that can ignite systemic change and drive us toward a future where the dignity and voice of every individual are not only recognized but are integral to the very fabric of our public policy.

CHAPTER 4

Voices from the Void: Communication and Connection in Government

4.1. Listening to the Silence: Understanding Unspoken Needs

The essence of communication lies not just in the spoken word, but also in the silence between those words — the unarticulated needs and the stories untold. In the government's vast machinery, these silences can be deafening, harboring the unspoken struggles and unmet needs of citizens and civil servants alike. It's in these voids that we find the opportunity to foster a deeper connection and cultivate a culture of attentiveness that can drive transformative changes in policy and administration.

The concept of 'listening to the silence' may seem abstract, yet it holds a profound significance for public servants. It implies an understanding of what is not being said — an awareness of the gaps between policies and their impacts, between services and the needs they are meant to satisfy. In this space, the silent voices are as critical as the vocal ones, and understanding them requires a heightened level of empathy and a deliberate effort to seek out those who have remained unheard.

A study in the 'American Review of Public Administration' found that nearly 30% of citizens who experienced dissatisfaction with public services never filed a complaint. Their reasons range from the belief that it would not make a difference to fear of the consequences.[60] These unvoiced concerns represent a vast reservoir of insight into the shortcomings and potential areas for improvement within public systems. They are an implicit call to action, prompting us to ask: How many signals are we missing because we haven't learned to interpret the silence?

I propose a shift in how we approach communication within government sectors. It starts with recognizing that unspoken needs are often the result of a lack of accessible channels for expression. Public institutions must develop more intuitive, less intimidating ways for individuals to communicate their experiences and needs. This could involve using technology to create anonymous feedback mechanisms or establishing community liaisons tasked with bringing forward the concerns of those less likely to engage directly with bureaucratic systems.

Yet, technology and formal systems alone will not suffice. There must be a concerted effort to cultivate what I call 'narrative awareness' — a skill set that enables public servants to read between the lines of community interactions and policy feedback. Narrative awareness involves actively seeking out the stories that lie beneath the surface, probing for understanding and genuinely engaging with the subtext of community discourse. It is about being present in the community, participating in its rhythms, and being open to the insights that emerge from simply being among the people we serve.

This concept is not without precedent. In Scandinavian countries, for instance, 'ombudsmen' — independent officers appointed to investigate individuals' complaints against maladministration — are standard. They serve as a bridge between the silent voices and the ears of the government. This model, while not perfect, demonstrates an institutional recognition of the importance of reaching into the silence to find those who have been marginalized by the cacophony of formal processes.

Training in empathetic listening should be part of the core curriculum for public servants. This training can incorporate lessons from social work, counseling, and community organizing, fields where listening to what is not being said is a fundamental skill. For example, role-playing exercises can help budding civil servants learn to pick up on non-verbal cues and practice reflective listening techniques that encourage openness and trust.

To foster a culture of listening within public institutions, leaders must set the tone. When leaders model attentive behavior, it sets an expectation for the organization. Leaders can host regular open forums, roundtable discussions, and listening sessions that not only invite spoken input but also give space for those who might not speak up. They can promote an environment where 'whistleblowers' and dissenting voices are protected and valued rather than marginalized and silenced.

The path forward requires a radical shift in our bureaucratic ethos. We must pivot from a culture of response to one of proactive engagement, venturing beyond the comfort of our offices and into the communities we serve. In these community spaces, the practice of participatory observation — being present without the pressure to immediately fix or respond — becomes invaluable. Here, public servants can learn the context of silence. A mother's hesitation in answering a question about school services may reveal her uncertainty about her child's educational future. A senior's reluctance to make eye contact may speak volumes about their isolation or past negative experiences with government officials. Each unspoken word adds to the tapestry of silent testimonies that, if heeded, can radically alter our approach to governance.

Incorporating these silent testimonies into policy-making requires an integrative approach. Data analytics, while powerful, must be complemented by qualitative insights gathered from the streets, from community centers, and from the quiet corners where the disenfranchised congregate. By synthesizing numerical data with the rich, often untapped qualitative data from these silent spaces, policies can be designed with a more holistic understanding of the people they impact.

Moreover, this engagement must not be sporadic; it needs to be sustained. Continuous feedback loops that capture both the voiced and unvoiced citizen feedback should be woven into the fabric of public service. Government workers at every level should be tasked with regular 'listening assignments,' prompting them to engage with different segments of the population and report back not just the content of the discussions, but also the context, the nonverbal cues, and the emotional undercurrents.

To this end, interdepartmental collaboration becomes paramount. Silos within government can stifle the flow of information and impede the kind of holistic listening required to discern unspoken needs. Sharing insights across departments can help create a 360-degree view of the citizen experience, breaking down the barriers to understanding that often result from compartmentalized structures.

Such an approach is not without challenges. It demands time, resources, and a shift in mindset. However, the potential rewards are immense. Engaging with the silent needs of the populace can lead to innovative services that anticipate issues before they become crises, policies that are more finely tuned to the realities of the lives they affect, and a government that is viewed not as an imposing authority but as a responsive ally in the pursuit of the common good.

Public service is a vocation grounded in the desire to make a difference. By honing our skills in listening to the silence, we affirm the dignity of those we serve and honor the responsibility entrusted to us. Through this practice, we do not merely administer services; we nurture the very fabric of our democracy, stitching together the disparate voices into a cohesive narrative that propels our nation forward. It is in the silent spaces that we often find the keys to unlock the most profound forms of progress, innovation, and connection that true public service aspires to achieve.

Section Coaching:

In the realms of government and public service, the act of listening extends far beyond the spoken word; it involves a keen attunement to the silent undercurrents of society. The ability to understand these unspoken needs is a critical skill for anyone involved in the machinery of governance. It is about observing beyond the obvious, hearing what is not said, and sensing the pulse of the unarticulated concerns of the populace. To listen to the silence is to acknowledge that what is omitted often carries as much weight as what is communicated.

Here is a nuanced approach to embracing this profound aspect of communication:

Cultivate Empathy: Begin with empathy, the cornerstone of effective public service. Empathetic listening requires an open heart and mind, freeing oneself from preconceptions and biases to truly understand the experiences and emotions of others.

Foster Accessibility: Create multiple, accessible channels for feedback, especially for those who may feel marginalized or unheard. This could involve community outreach programs, suggestion boxes, social media platforms, and other informal means that encourage open communication.

Practice Active Observation: Active observation involves being present within communities and paying attention to non-verbal cues. It's about reading between the lines of what citizens do, what they prioritize, and what concerns them in their day-to-day lives.

Engage in Reflective Silence: Allocate time for silence in conversations, allowing space for thoughts and feelings to emerge. Reflective silence can be more telling than pressured speech, offering a gateway to deeper understanding.

Encourage Whistleblowing: Protect and value the voices that dare to speak up about systemic issues. These often start as silent concerns that, when given the right environment, can lead to significant insights and reforms.

Provide Anonymity Where Needed: Sometimes the freedom to speak without attribution can draw out silent voices. Anonymous feedback mechanisms can be instrumental in uncovering hidden challenges within systems.

Utilize Narrative Inquiry: Employ narrative inquiry as a tool to explore the stories and lived experiences of individuals and communities. It's a qualitative approach that delves into the personal accounts that shape public perception and experience.

Offer Empathetic Response Training: Equip public servants with the skills to respond empathetically to both spoken and unspoken messages. Trainings should focus on emotional intelligence, non-verbal communication, and cultural sensitivity.

Encourage Community Liaisons: Community liaisons can serve as the ears of the government within the populace, translating unspoken needs into actionable insights that can inform policy and practice.

Integrate Feedback Loops: Establish continuous feedback loops that not only capture direct responses but also monitor the broader socio-cultural indicators that reflect the unspoken needs and values of the community.

By mastering the art of listening to the silence, public servants can transform the landscape of public service. This holistic approach to communication ensures that every citizen is heard, every concern is valued, and every solution is crafted with a deep understanding of the silent narratives that drive societal dynamics. This silent dialogue, when harnessed effectively, can be the catalyst for innovative policies and profound change within the public sector.

4.2 Communicating Across the Divide: Building Bridges in Fragmented Systems

In the heart of governance, communication serves as the vital lifeline that connects the myriad limbs of public service. Yet, in a paradox of modern bureaucracy, as systems grow more comprehensive, they also become more compartmentalized. Fragmented systems, therefore, pose a peculiar challenge: how to build bridges across the gaps that inhibit not just the flow of information but also the spirit of cooperation necessary for holistic governance. This phenomenon is akin to constructing a vast network of highways without on-ramps and off-ramps; there is connectivity potential, but it remains unrealized without deliberate design to link disparate paths.

Building these bridges is not an endeavor of engineering; it is an act of empathy, strategy, and relentless commitment to public service. It requires an understanding of both the art of human connection and the science of effective communication. To navigate these often treacherous waters, one must employ a compass that aligns with both heart and mind, guided by the constellations of data and personal insight. This alignment enables leaders to craft a shared narrative that resonates with every member of their organization, creating a cohesive vision that traverses organizational divides.

Interdepartmental Synergy through Empathetic Leadership: Empathy in leadership is a cornerstone for interdepartmental synergy. Empathetic leaders have the unique capability to understand the perspectives, needs, and challenges of various departments. By fostering a culture where empathy is valued, leaders can break down the walls of miscommunication and mistrust that often exist between departments. This emotional intelligence within leadership is not merely a soft skill but a strategic asset. A survey conducted by the Center for Creative Leadership found that managers who show more empathy toward their direct reports are viewed as better performers by their boss. Additionally, empathy builds a foundation for authentic connections, enabling leaders to not only share but also to shape the collective experience of their teams, carving out a space where every voice is heard and valued.

Strategic Storytelling to Forge Common Ground: Strategic storytelling is a powerful tool for building bridges. It is the act of sharing experiences, challenges, and successes in a narrative form to illustrate common values and goals. By articulating a vision through stories, leaders can connect individuals across departments on an emotional level, fostering a shared understanding that transcends the written policy or directive. In the realm of government, where policies can often seem abstract, storytelling puts a human face to the effects of bureaucratic decision-making. The National Storytelling Network highlights that stories have the power to prompt action and make complex issues more accessible and relatable. Through stories, the abstract becomes tangible, and the impersonal becomes personal, thus transforming policy from a directive into a dialogue.

Data-Driven Decision-Making to Support Communication: Data-driven decision-making underpins effective communication strategies. In fragmented systems, the challenge often lies in not just the availability of data but in its interpretation and the communication of its implications. By harnessing the power of data analytics, government leaders can identify communication gaps and tailor their strategies to bridge these divides. For instance, data can reveal the frequency of interdepartmental interactions, helping to identify which connections are underdeveloped and why. This analytical approach, when coupled with an empathetic understanding of the data's human element, allows leaders to make informed decisions that acknowledge the complex interplay between numbers and narratives.

Cultivating Cross-Pollination through Technology: The digital era offers unprecedented opportunities for cross-pollination between departments. Platforms like Slack and Microsoft Teams have revolutionized the way colleagues can interact, collaborate, and break down silos. A study from the Journal of Knowledge Management suggests that social technologies, when fully integrated into the workflow, can raise the productivity of high-skill knowledge workers by 20 to 25 percent.[61] This technological integration can catalyze a new era of interdepartmental communication where ideas flow freely, and silos are dismantled not by mandate, but through the organic interactions of a digitally empowered workforce.

Creating Forums for Cross-Departmental Collaboration: Creating forums for collaboration can be as literal as organizing interdepartmental meetings or as innovative as setting up internal 'innovation labs' where individuals from different departments can come together to solve common problems. These forums serve as a breeding ground for ideas and can be the first step towards a more integrated approach to public service. They offer safe spaces for risk-taking and innovation, where the fear of failure is replaced with the thrill of exploration and the potential for collective achievement.

Measuring Impact to Guide Communication Efforts: Finally, it is critical to measure the impact of communication efforts. This could mean tracking the number of collaborative projects between departments, the frequency and quality of interdepartmental communications, or employee satisfaction rates. By setting KPIs around communication, organizations can ensure that their efforts to bridge the divide are not just well-intentioned but effective. These metrics serve as the feedback loop that informs and refines the communication strategy, ensuring that it evolves to meet the changing dynamics of the organization.

In essence, communicating across the divide in fragmented systems requires a multifaceted approach, blending empathy, data, and technology with the timeless art of storytelling. It is an approach that seeks not to overpower the complexities of bureaucracy but to navigate them with a spirit of unity and a focus on common goals. As we embrace this approach, the void that once echoed with missed connections and unspoken needs can become a space vibrant with the voices of collaboration and innovation, transforming the landscape of public service into a dynamic tapestry woven from the threads of countless narratives, data points, and digital exchanges.

4.3 Authentic Voices: How Personal Truths Can Influence Public Discourse

The heart of public service beats to the rhythm of individual narratives, each with its unique melody and timbre. These authentic voices in governance hold immense potential to penetrate the bastions of power, resonate within the complex networks of policy-making, and mold the discourse that shapes the contours of public life. When personal truths are embraced in the public realm, they have the transformative power to cut through the noise of overused platitudes and ignite genuine connection, spurring significant reform and evolution within society.

The Power of Personal Narratives: In an increasingly data-driven world, personal narratives offer a unique means of connection, grounding high-level discussions in the lived experiences of individuals. These stories are not just supplementary; they are central to the human condition. The empirical evidence supporting the efficacy of storytelling in changing hearts and minds is substantial. When integrated into the public sphere, these narratives serve as a critical lever, moving the behemoth of bureaucracy with the compelling force of authenticity.

Bridging Policy and Personal Experience: The convergence of personal experience with policy articulation serves to demystify governmental processes. By sharing personal stakes in policy matters, legislators transform abstract propositions into relatable narratives. This narrative infusion breathes life into the skeletal structure of policies, adding flesh, blood, and beating hearts to otherwise static documents. It's a dynamic that not only humanizes lawmakers in the eyes of their electorate but also fosters a deeper, more profound understanding of the policies they advocate.

Cultivating Authenticity in Government Communication: Authentic government communication is an antidote to the alienation many feel from the bureaucratic processes that shape their lives. It invites a shift from detached formalism to narratives steeped in the reality of everyday experiences. When communication strategies incorporate vulnerability and share narratives reflective of the populace, they do more than disseminate information—they build rapport and foster a sense of shared stakeholding in societal outcomes.

Personal Truths as Catalysts for Change: Stories of personal challenges and triumphs told by government officials can serve as potent catalysts for legislative and social change. These personal accounts provide more than just a human element; they offer a compelling case for the necessity of policy reform. Such stories can break through political impasses and contribute to the momentum needed to overcome entrenched barriers to change, ensuring that legislation is not only reactive but also proactive in improving citizens' lives.

Authentic Voices in Constituent Engagement: Constituents, when armed with their personal stories, have the power to influence policy-making profoundly. The personalization of constituent communication humanizes the abstract nature of legislation and regulation, imbuing them with the urgency of real-world impact. This engagement transforms passive observation into active participation, turning constituents into powerful narrators of their collective destiny.

Leveraging Diversity of Voices: Incorporating a kaleidoscope of personal narratives from diverse demographics ensures that policies are not only crafted with equity in mind but also with a richness that can only come from a plurality of perspectives. This approach leads to a more holistic and sensitive policy environment, one that respects and acknowledges the varied tapestry of the human experience.

Authentic Voices as a Learning Tool: The internal culture of government institutions is also deeply enriched by the sharing of personal stories. Such narratives encourage a culture of continuous learning and understanding, enabling civil servants to gain insight into the multifaceted lives of the citizens they serve. This narrative-sharing approach can break down institutional silos, fostering a more collaborative and empathetic workspace.

The resonance of authentic voices within the sphere of public service is undeniable. These narratives are more than mere anecdotes; they are the lifeblood of a responsive and adaptive government. The exchange of personal truths not only fosters greater transparency and authenticity but also serves as the bedrock for trust between the governed and those who govern. By weaving the diverse threads of individual experiences into the fabric of governance, leaders and lawmakers can ensure that the edifice of public service is not only strong and just but also deeply human. As the call for genuine engagement in governance grows louder, the power of authentic narratives stands as a testament to the enduring importance of personal truths in the collective journey toward a more empathetic and effective democracy.

CHAPTER 5

Leading with Heart: Emotionally Intelligent Governance

5.1 The Power of Vulnerability in Leadership

The traditional bastion of government, often perceived as an impenetrable fortress of stoicism and impersonal decree, is undergoing a transformative reckoning. With society's growing appetite for authenticity and emotional intelligence, the valorization of vulnerability in leadership has ascended to become a force of undeniable impact. This section delves deeply into the seemingly paradoxical strength inherent in vulnerability, illustrating through vivid examples and scholarly evidence how it can galvanize teams, foster trust, and ultimately lead to more effective governance. It is an exploration of how governmental leadership, once cloaked in the veneer of infallibility, is finding resounding resonance in the power of shared human experience.

Vulnerability in the realm of leadership is a journey from the armor of invincibility to the courage of transparency about one's feelings, doubts, and experiences. Dr. Brené Brown, whose work has become a cornerstone in understanding vulnerability, suggests it is the birthplace of innovation, creativity, and change. When leaders embrace their vulnerability, they forge a path of empathy and connection, signaling to constituents and colleagues alike that it is not only safe to do so but that it is essential for collective growth. This cultural metamorphosis can bring to life the nuanced complexities of leading with emotion, ensuring that governance is not a sterile execution of tasks but a human-centered endeavor.

The correlation between emotionally intelligent leadership and positive organizational outcomes is supported by a substantial body of research. For example, a study by the Organization Development Journal reveals that companies with emotionally intelligent leaders enjoy increased productivity and profitability, and notably, these leaders instill a culture that significantly reduces turnover rates.[62] These findings underscore the profound impact that emotionally attuned leadership can have, not just on the bottom line, but on the vibrancy and sustainability of the workforce. The data compels us to consider how the integration of emotional intelligence into leadership training could serve as a transformative agent within the public sector.

In the crucible of crisis management, the true power of vulnerability comes into sharp relief. Consider the global tumult created by the COVID-19 pandemic: leaders who communicated with transparency, who admitted uncertainties, and shared their emotional challenges fostered a strong sense of community and shared purpose. This sense of solidarity, born from the vulnerability of leaders, becomes a powerful conduit for building trust, driving collaboration, and mobilizing concerted action—a stark contrast to those leaders who remain ensconced behind a façade of unwavering certainty.

Yet, the embrace of vulnerability is not devoid of risks and necessitates a supportive environment where openness is not exploited but cherished. Cultivating a culture that venerates vulnerability requires a concerted effort, beginning with leaders who embody and advocate for this approach. The implementation of emotional intelligence training programs becomes crucial in this cultural shift, providing leaders with the toolkit to navigate the complexities of their own vulnerabilities and to respond to those of their colleagues with sensitivity and comprehension.

Leaders fostering emotional intelligence are tasked with a delicate balancing act—harnessing vulnerability with discernment. It is about strategically choosing moments of openness that constructively contribute to building relationships and furthering the mission of the organization. Emotional intelligence thus becomes a potent adjunct to the decision-making process, augmenting it with a profound depth of human insight.

The ripple effects of leading with heart and vulnerability extend to policy-making, ushering in an era of governance that is more inclusive and responsive to the varied tapestry of societal needs. This inclusivity amplifies the relevance and impact of policies and, in doing so, fortifies the foundation of public trust in governmental institutions.

As the narrative of modern governance continues to evolve, the clarion call for leaders who can navigate its complexities with heart and emotional intelligence becomes increasingly resonant. By embracing the transformative power of vulnerability, leaders have the capacity to dismantle barriers, engendering a more interconnected relationship between government entities and the public they serve. The insights and evidence presented here advocate for vulnerability as a cornerstone of emotionally intelligent governance. As we turn our attention to the next section on building emotionally bonded teams, the journey of integrating heart into the leadership fabric of public service is affirmed as not just challenging but deeply rewarding, signifying a paradigm shift that could redefine the future of governance.

Section Coaching:

Embracing vulnerability in leadership, especially within the structured confines of government, can be a formidable challenge. However, the power of vulnerability is an untapped force that can lead to stronger connections, increased trust, and a more cohesive team dynamic.

Emotional Intelligence and Vulnerability

Emotional intelligence (EI) is the ability to understand and manage your own emotions and those of others. For leaders, high EI is essential for recognizing their own vulnerability and using it to connect with their team on a human level. Leaders with high EI are adept at emotional regulation, demonstrate empathy, and are skilled in navigating interpersonal dynamics within their teams.

Creating a Culture of Trust

Vulnerability fosters trust—a crucial element in any leader's relationship with their team. When leaders are open about challenges, uncertainties, and personal setbacks, it humanizes them and makes them more relatable. This openness encourages team members to share their own ideas and concerns without fear of judgment or retribution.

Encouraging Open Communication

Leaders who are vulnerable create an environment where open communication is the norm. This is particularly important in government, where the stakes are high, and the impact of decisions is widespread. Encouraging open communication means actively listening to feedback, acknowledging different perspectives, and admitting when one doesn't have all the answers.

Leading by Example

When leaders show vulnerability, they set a precedent for their team to do the same. This can lead to a more collaborative and innovative work environment. Leaders who admit to mistakes or gaps in their knowledge demonstrate that taking risks and learning from failure is a valued part of the organizational culture.

Balancing Vulnerability and Authority

It's important for leaders to balance their vulnerability with maintaining their authority. This balance can be struck by showing confidence in the face of uncertainty and providing clear direction even when admitting to not having all the answers. The key is to be authentic and not use vulnerability as a tactic, but rather as a genuine expression of one's leadership style.

The Role of Vulnerability in Policymaking

Vulnerability can also play a significant role in policymaking. Leaders who acknowledge the limits of their understanding can be more open to input from a diverse range of sources, leading to policies that are more reflective of the community's needs. This approach also allows for flexibility and adaptability in policy implementation.

Vulnerability in leadership, particularly within the government sector, can transform the way teams and organizations operate. It can break down barriers, foster innovation, and create a work environment that is conducive to growth and change. By embracing vulnerability, leaders in government can inspire their teams, build trust, and lead more effectively. As we transition to the next topic of building emotional bonds within the workplace, it's important to remember that vulnerability is not a weakness but a compelling leadership strength that can lead to a more engaged and resilient public service.

5.2. Teams with Heart: Building Emotional Bonds in the Workplace

In the preceding chapter, we explored the crucial role of vulnerability in leadership. Now we turn our focus to the collective—how emotional intelligence can nurture not only the individual leader but the entire team, fostering emotional bonds that transform the workplace from a mere setting of transactional interactions into a dynamic ecosystem pulsating with shared purpose and mutual support.

The concept of a team with heart might seem intangible, even sentimental, in the cut-and-dry world of bureaucracy, yet it is the very essence of a functional and thriving public sector organization. Emotional bonds are the sinew that binds the team, allowing for the flow of creativity, collaboration, and compassion necessary to navigate the complex and often challenging landscape of public service. This section will illuminate the process of building these bonds and provide practical strategies for infusing the workplace with emotional intelligence.

A Harvard Business Review article emphasized the importance of empathy in teams, citing it as a non-negotiable for leaders who want to maximize productivity and retain talent.[63] A study from the Center for Creative Leadership also found that managers who show more empathy toward direct reports are viewed as better performers by their boss.[64] These findings underscore the quantifiable benefits of fostering an emotionally connected team.

Building emotional bonds in the workplace begins with active listening. When team members feel heard, they are more engaged. This does not mean simply waiting for one's turn to speak, but rather, seeking to understand the emotions and intentions behind the words. In government work, where the consequences of actions can be far-reaching, listening can translate to policies that resonate more deeply with the public because they are rooted in genuine comprehension of needs.

Emotionally charged situations are inevitable. How we handle conflict can make or break the emotional bonds within a team. Instead of viewing disagreement as a disruption, we can reframe it as an opportunity to strengthen relationships. Conflict resolution strategies that focus on emotional intelligence, such as those espoused by the Harvard Negotiation Project, encourage finding the emotions at the heart of the conflict and addressing those, not just the surface issue.

Another pivotal element is the recognition and celebration of individual and team accomplishments. This goes beyond the occasional 'Employee of the Month' award to a more nuanced appreciation of the unique contributions each person makes. Celebrating milestones, acknowledging personal efforts, and even understanding the personal hardships of team members contribute to a culture where individuals feel valued not just for what they do but for who they are.

To integrate these principles into the fabric of a bureaucratic institution, it's critical to look at the structural supports that are in place. This includes policies that allow for flexible work arrangements, emphasizing work-life balance, and providing access to mental health resources. Google's Aristotle Project, which studied hundreds of its teams, found that the most important factor to a successful team was psychological safety—a sense of confidence that the team will not embarrass, reject, or punish someone for speaking up.

Yet, building a team with heart is not a set-and-forget initiative. It requires ongoing effort and must be nurtured through regular team-building activities, retreats, and open forums for feedback. These initiatives provide a space for team members to step away from the day-to-day tasks and engage with each other on a more personal level, thereby deepening emotional bonds.

There must be a recognition that building emotional bonds is an evolving process, one that adapts to the shifting landscapes of public service and the personal growth of its members. It's not about creating a utopian workplace where conflict doesn't exist but about cultivating an environment where the team can navigate those conflicts with understanding, empathy, and a shared commitment to the collective good.

Teams with heart are the lifeblood of emotionally intelligent governance. As we have seen, the benefits of nurturing these bonds are profound, resulting in not just happier employees, but more effective, resilient, and compassionate public service. This section has laid the groundwork for understanding how such teams can be cultivated, offering actionable insights and strategies that can be implemented to create a workplace where emotional intelligence is not an afterthought but a fundamental characteristic of the organizational culture. As we proceed, we will look into real-world case studies that exemplify leaders who have successfully changed the bureaucratic landscape through emotionally intelligent governance.

Section Coaching:

Building emotional bonds within a team, particularly in a government setting where procedures and formality often take center stage, is essential for creating an environment where employees feel valued and connected. In this section we focused on the strategies and practices that foster these vital connections, turning a group of individuals into a cohesive and supportive unit capable of exceptional service and collaboration.

Active Listening and Empathetic Engagement
The foundation of any strong relationship is communication, and within teams, this starts with active listening. Active listening goes beyond just hearing words; it involves engaging with empathy, asking thoughtful questions, and responding with consideration. When team members feel genuinely heard, it creates a sense of belonging and trust, which are cornerstones of a strong emotional bond.

Conflict as a Catalyst for Strengthening Bonds
Conflict is inevitable in any team but navigating these disagreements with emotional intelligence can actually strengthen team dynamics. Leaders should foster an environment where differing opinions are respected and where constructive conflict resolution practices are the norm. Teams that can successfully navigate conflict often emerge with stronger mutual respect and a deeper understanding of one another.

Recognition and Appreciation
Regularly recognizing and celebrating both individual achievements and team milestones contributes significantly to building emotional bonds. Recognition should be personalized, sincere, and specific, highlighting not just the accomplishments but also the qualities and efforts of the individuals involved.

Flexible and Supportive Work Policies
Institutional support is critical for emotional bonding within teams. This includes creating policies that promote work-life balance, like flexible working hours, and providing resources for mental and emotional well-being. Such policies demonstrate an organization's commitment to the holistic well-being of its employees, which, in turn, nurtures emotional bonds.

Team-Building Initiatives
Team-building activities should not be a once-a-year event but a regular part of the team's operation. These initiatives can range from informal lunch gatherings to structured workshops, all designed to allow team

members to interact in settings outside of their regular work tasks. These interactions can lead to a deeper understanding and appreciation of each team member's unique personality and life outside of work.

Psychological Safety
Creating a psychologically safe environment where team members can speak up without fear of embarrassment or retribution is essential. This sense of safety encourages risk-taking and honesty, which are key to innovation and problem-solving within teams.

Sustaining Emotional Bonds
Maintaining emotional bonds requires ongoing effort. Leaders should check in regularly with their teams, not just about work-related issues but about their general well-being. Open forums for feedback and discussions about the team's emotional climate should be encouraged.

Building teams with heart is about creating a work culture that values emotional connections as much as it does professional achievements. It's about understanding that these bonds are the undercurrents that drive team success and satisfaction. By implementing the strategies discussed here, leaders can cultivate teams that are not only productive but also supportive and engaged, embodying the ethos of emotionally intelligent governance. As we delve into the next section, we will see these principles in action and explore the profound impact emotional bonds can have on transforming government work environments.

5.3. Case Studies: Leaders Who Changed the Bureaucracy

The journey through the heart of change in governance is incomplete without living examples. The leaders profiled here embody the profound impact that emotional intelligence (EI) can have in reforming and revitalizing bureaucratic systems. Their stories illustrate how, when harnessed correctly, EI can not only influence policy and practice but can also instill a sense of purpose and connection in organizations often perceived as rigid and impersonal.

Prime Minister Jacinda Ardern of New Zealand became a paragon of empathetic leadership in times of turmoil. Her response to the Christchurch mosque shootings was marked by an unprecedented show of solidarity and compassion. Ardern didn't just offer thoughts and prayers; she donned a hijab, stood with the families in mourning, and swiftly moved to change gun laws. Similarly, during the COVID-19 pandemic, her government's approach was characterized by clear, compassionate communication and policies that prioritized the well-being of citizens over economic concerns. The financial subsidies introduced were a testament to a governance model that measures success not only by the wealth of a nation but by the health and happiness of its people. Under her guidance, New Zealand not only flattened the curve rapidly but also nurtured a sense of unity and collective responsibility.

In education, the remarkable efforts of Dr. Nadia Lopez shine brightly. As the founder of Mott Hall Bridges Academy, her leadership transcended conventional academic goals. Lopez understood that emotional intelligence is not a luxury but a necessity, especially in low-income areas where children face myriad challenges. Her vision led to a curriculum that integrates emotional support with academic rigor, ensuring that students are seen, heard, and nurtured. This approach to education—viewing students holistically rather than as test scores—has redefined success for the community of Brownsville, turning the school into a beacon of hope and a model for educational reform across the country.

Satya Nadella's transformation of Microsoft's culture from cutthroat competition to one of empathy and collaboration is a testament to the power of EI in corporate leadership. Nadella inspired a sense of purpose and belonging among employees, fostering a culture where learning from failure is encouraged and personal growth is as valued as professional achievement. This pivot was not just morally sound; it paid dividends, as evidenced by Microsoft's market resurgence. His leadership underscores the idea that businesses can thrive when they create environments where innovation is fueled by a workforce that feels supported and valued.

The late Tony Hsieh of Zappos brought a novel ethos to corporate America with his emphasis on happiness as a business strategy. Hsieh's approach went beyond traditional metrics of customer satisfaction; he built a company culture where employees' emotional well-being was a priority. The result was a loyal workforce and a beloved brand, proving that emotional intelligence can drive success in even the most profit-driven industries.

On the front lines of public safety, Chief Chris Magnus's tenure in Richmond, California, and Tucson, Arizona, highlights how EI can transform law enforcement. Magnus's community policing strategies, which replaced traditional force with empathy and outreach, significantly decreased crime rates and fostered community trust. His policies show that treating the public with dignity and respect is not only the right thing to do but also the most effective.

Chancellor Angela Merkel of Germany demonstrated emotional intelligence on an international stage, particularly during the European migrant crisis. Merkel's decision to welcome refugees was a striking example of leadership that balances head and heart, showing that policy can be both practical and compassionate. Her leadership style, often balancing rationality with empathy, has shown that even within the complex arena of geopolitics, emotional intelligence is a vital tool for navigating the multifaceted challenges of the modern world.

These leaders represent the vanguard of emotionally intelligent governance. Their achievements reinforce the notion that compassion and empathy are powerful levers for change, capable of moving the gears of bureaucracy in a direction that uplifts and unites. The long-term impact of their leadership is a testament to the effectiveness of EI in fostering an environment of respect, creativity, and progress. They have not only redefined the parameters of their respective offices but also laid down the emotional and ethical foundations for those who will follow in their footsteps.

Embracing the full spectrum of human capabilities in leadership, the case studies highlighted in Chapter 5 stand as enduring exemplars of emotionally intelligent governance. Each leader, with their unique approach to the challenges of their sectors, demonstrates that leadership is as much about the heart as it is about the mind. The concept of leading with heart—evident in the stories of Ardern, Lopez, Nadella, Hsieh, Magnus, and Merkel—is a potent reminder that when governance is infused with empathy, compassion, and emotional awareness, it transcends traditional expectations and metrics of success.

Jacinda Ardern's leadership illustrates the transformative power of empathy in action. The way she galvanized New Zealand to come together in the wake of tragedy, fostering a culture of inclusivity and unity, epitomizes emotionally intelligent governance. Ardern's approach, which we delved into earlier, went beyond symbolic gestures; it ushered in substantive policy shifts that reflected a deep understanding of her constituents' needs.

Dr. Nadia Lopez's pioneering work in education underscores the significant role emotional intelligence plays in shaping the future of young minds. By forging an educational environment that caters to the emotional and academic needs of students, Lopez has demonstrated that the heart of educational reform lies in recognizing the humanity of each student. The nurturing atmosphere at Mott Hall Bridges Academy, detailed previously, stands as a microcosm of what is possible when educational leaders value the inner lives of their students as much as their academic performance.

Satya Nadella's influence at Microsoft reshaped a corporate giant, proving that a culture of empathy can yield remarkable results. Nadella's commitment to a growth mindset, as we explored, transformed Microsoft's ethos, encouraging innovation and collaboration. His tenure is a clear indication that emotional intelligence in leadership is not just about individual interactions but about cultivating an environment where every employee can contribute to their fullest potential.

Tony Hsieh's vision for Zappos transformed the customer service industry. By valuing employee happiness and empowerment, Hsieh created an unparalleled corporate culture that achieved extraordinary customer loyalty and satisfaction. The success of Zappos, as we've seen, is a testament to the efficacy of emotionally intelligent business practices and their impact on both employees and customers.

In the arena of public safety, Chief Chris Magnus's adoption of community policing practices reflects a profound shift in law enforcement. His methods, based on emotional intelligence, acknowledge the humanity within communities, resulting in decreased crime rates and improved police-community relations, as we previously acknowledged. Magnus's leadership exemplifies how empathy and respect can redefine the role of law enforcement in society.

Angela Merkel's governance, particularly during the migrant crisis, demonstrated a remarkable blend of practical decision-making and moral leadership. Merkel's policies were characterized by a compassionate pragmatism that resonated on a global scale, illustrating how emotional intelligence can influence international policy and affect global change.

Each of these leaders exhibits an understanding that emotionally intelligent governance is not a fleeting trend but a fundamental shift in leadership philosophy. They showcase how leaders can harness emotional insights to inspire, innovate, and drive progress. Their stories, as discussed, are not just narratives of personal achievement; they are blueprints for how to integrate emotional intelligence into the fabric of governance.

Emotional intelligence, as demonstrated by these leaders, is an indispensable ingredient in the alchemy of leadership. It's a resource that, when genuinely understood and skillfully applied, can redefine the possible within bureaucratic systems. These narratives serve not just as portraits of effective leadership but as a dynamic map for infusing our institutions with the kind of heartfelt governance that elevates the human spirit alongside the collective goals.

CHAPTER 6

Innovating with Integrity: Personal Conviction and Professional Duty

6.1. The Innovator's Dilemma: Staying True to Oneself While Navigating Red Tape

Within the heart of every public sector innovator, there exists a harmonious yet often conflicting melody. The steady, methodical beat of bureaucracy pulsates in the background, setting a rhythm of regulation and routine. In counterpoint, the quickened pulse of progress thrums with the vibrant potential of change and modernization. This is the symphony of the innovator's existence—the perpetual oscillation between the known and the unknown, the safe harbor of tradition and the uncharted seas of advancement. They are the visionaries who perceive beyond the horizon of the present, daring to draft blueprints of a future that can be if only the shackles of "the way we've always done it" are cast off.

This dance—the innovator's dilemma—is an intricate ballet, one that requires an acute sense of timing and an unerring ability to step to the rhythms of both continuity and change. The innovator within the public sector must not only conceive ideas that sparkle with potential but also navigate the dense fog of regulation that can obscure the path to realization. They must employ their personal convictions as beacons, casting light upon innovative pathways that might otherwise remain hidden in the bureaucratic mist. The journey they embark upon is not selected for ease or comfort; rather, it is a path chosen out of a deep-seated understanding that without their courage and commitment to change, the machinery of government risks becoming an artifact, a relic incapable of serving the evolving needs of the citizenry.

The evidence in favor of innovation within the public sector is compelling and unequivocal. Data echoes the stark reality that without the oxygen of fresh ideas and novel approaches, the body politic suffers, trust diminishes, and the collective goodwill of the populace towards their government dissipates. A Research Policy study paints this picture clearly, indicating that governmental bodies that resist the tide of innovation do not simply stagnate; they recede in the esteem of those they serve, experiencing a marked drop in public satisfaction.[65] These entities become like still water, and in the absence of the currents of innovation, they grow brackish and unwholesome.

Public sector innovators, therefore, are more than mere employees within a system; they are its vital force, the catalysts of progress that prevent the sclerosis of institutional inertia. These are the bold individuals who challenge the status quo, who look at the leviathan of government and see not an immovable object but a puzzle awaiting a solution, a maze ripe for navigation. By embedding their convictions within the bedrock of bureaucracy, they do not simply move within the system—they move the system itself.[66]

The public sector innovator embodies a unique brand of heroism. They recognize that the path they choose is fraught with challenges and that the map they draw is one that others may be reluctant to follow. Yet they persist, for in their heart beats the conviction that their efforts are not just for the betterment of the systems they inhabit, but for the society that system serves. The dance of innovation within government is an enduring one, and its participants are those who hold fast to the belief that progress, no matter how encumbered by the weight of red tape and regulation, is not only possible—it is essential.

The challenge then becomes one of translation—how does one convert the language of personal conviction into the lexicon of bureaucratic success? The journey is complex, but history and experience have furnished a set of guiding principles and strategies that, when applied with finesse, can yield substantial progress:

Navigating Red Tape with Personal Conviction: Navigating the thicket of red tape that often binds the mechanisms of government requires more than mere expertise; it demands an unwavering dedication to one's personal convictions. To infuse the monolithic structures of bureaucracy with innovation, public sector changemakers must be both compass and captain, steering their projects through the complex channels of policies and procedures. The 2020 Bloomberg Cities Network report sheds light on a compelling trend: initiatives born from the fire of personal passion and conviction are not only launched but also are more effectively woven into the ongoing narrative of government service

Articulate Your Vision Clearly: Communicate your innovative ideas in a manner that resonates with stakeholders. It is essential to articulate how these innovations align with the broader goals of the organization. A clear and compelling narrative that connects personal conviction to public good can bridge the gap between skepticism and support.

Foster Strategic Relationships: Building a network of allies who share your vision or stand to benefit from your innovation can amplify your efforts. These relationships can create a coalition that navigates bureaucracy more effectively, providing the collective weight needed to move initiatives forward.

Utilize Evidence-Based Advocacy: Arm yourself with data and case studies that underscore the efficacy and benefits of your proposals. Bureaucracies respect the power of evidence, and data-driven arguments can cut through layers of hesitation and resistance.

Embrace Incremental Progress: Small, calculated moves often underpin the success of innovative endeavors in the public sector. By securing quick wins and building on them, you can create a ripple effect, leading to larger waves of change over time.

Navigate with Political Savvy: Understanding the political landscape and the interests of various stakeholders can help you craft strategies that are both innovative and politically astute. This involves a balance of assertiveness and diplomacy to advance your projects without alienating potential allies.

Cultivate Resilience: The path of innovation is littered with obstacles. A resilient mindset allows you to weather setbacks and persist despite the slow pace of change. Resilience transforms barriers into stepping stones toward eventual success.

Engage in Continuous Learning: Bureaucratic systems are not static, and neither are the skills needed to navigate them. Continuously hone your knowledge of new policies, procedures, and political dynamics. This will enable you to adapt your strategies to the ever-changing landscape of government.

Leverage Regulatory Frameworks: Instead of viewing regulations as barriers, use them as scaffolds upon which to construct your innovative ideas. Show how your innovation operates within the bounds of regulation, or how it can inform the development of new regulatory frameworks.

Promote Transparency: Be open about your goals, the potential impact of your initiatives, and the challenges you face. Transparency fosters trust and can lead to unexpected support from within the bureaucracy.

Demonstrate Value: Ultimately, showcasing the tangible benefits of your innovation to the public and to government officials alike can secure the buy-in needed to sustain momentum. Value can be demonstrated through improved efficiencies, cost savings, better outcomes, or public approval.

By deploying these strategies with skill and conviction, public sector innovators can cut a clear path through the dense underbrush of bureaucracy. Their personal convictions become the very engine of progress, propelling their professional endeavors forward, not as antagonists to the established order, but as dynamic allies to the public good. Each small triumph is a testament to the transformative power of dedication and a step toward a future where government works not just efficiently, but with enlightened ingenuity.

Additional Innovators' Strategies

Building Coalitions of the Willing: In the sprawling networks of government bureaucracy, the adage "strength in numbers" takes on a strategic significance for innovators. The journey of an idea from inception to implementation is often a treacherous one, fraught with the pitfalls of policy, the quagmires of red tape, and the sometimes capricious winds of political will. It is within this complex ecosystem that building coalitions becomes not just useful, but essential. The innovation process, especially in the public sector, is a collective endeavor requiring a symphony of diverse voices and concerted efforts.

The task of forming a coalition begins with identifying potential allies. These are individuals who share a vision for change or who can recognize the value in an innovator's proposal. They may be found at various levels of the hierarchy and across different departments, creating a multidisciplinary tapestry that can approach problems from various angles and propose holistic solutions. Building these coalitions involves a careful blend of social acumen, strategic communication, and the cultivation of relationships based on mutual respect and common goals.

Once allies are identified, the next step is to foster these connections into a functioning, purposeful coalition. This requires regular communication, the establishment of shared objectives, and the alignment of different agendas towards a common aim. Each member of the coalition brings unique insights, resources, and access to the table, enriching the innovation process and empowering the group to navigate bureaucratic challenges more effectively than any individual could alone.

Evidence of the efficacy of such coalitions can be found in multiple case studies. Research shows that when innovators forge strategic alliances, their projects gain momentum, benefit from a diversity of perspectives, and can more swiftly adapt to the shifting landscapes of public administration. There is also a cumulative effect: as small successes are won, the coalition's influence grows, making it easier to attract additional supporters and to create a virtuous cycle of innovation and improvement.

A coalition of the willing does more than just push individual projects; it cultivates an environment where innovation can flourish. When a group of committed individuals advocates for change, they can gradually shift the culture of their organization, making it more receptive to new ideas. This cultural shift is pivotal—it's the soil in which future innovations will take root.

Moreover, such coalitions serve as a support system for its members. The path of innovation is often littered with obstacles and setbacks. A coalition provides a buffer against discouragement and a forum for strategizing around roadblocks. It can also be a source of moral support, reinforcing each member's commitment to their shared cause.

In practical terms, building a coalition may involve regular meetings, the creation of communication channels like newsletters or group chats, and the organization of workshops or brainstorming sessions. It also requires leadership—someone to coordinate efforts, keep the group focused, and represent the coalition's interests in larger organizational discussions.

Ultimately, building coalitions of the willing is about weaving a stronger fabric of innovation within the government. Each thread—each member of the coalition—strengthens the overall capacity to initiate and sustain meaningful change. These coalitions become the heart of the innovative spirit within bureaucracy, pumping vitality into the veins of public sector systems and ensuring that innovation is not an isolated incident but a standard practice. In this way, the coalition moves beyond mere collaboration, becoming a formidable force for progress and a beacon for others who wish to make their mark on the tapestry of government operations.

Understanding the Language of Bureaucracy: Navigating the realm of bureaucracy demands a fluency in its distinct language—a dialect comprised of regulations, procedures, and the ever-important jargon of compliance and risk management. For the innovator, the ability to speak this language is crucial, as it allows one to cloak the avant-garde in the familiar, transforming the radical into the acceptable and the new into the necessary.

The art of narrative reframing is not simply about choosing the right words; it is about aligning one's vision of change with the core values and mandates of the institution. Innovators adept in this art can craft compelling stories that weave their proposals into the existing organizational tapestry. They turn their ideas into narratives that resonate with the deep-seated principles of the bureaucracy, such as due diligence, cost efficiency, and accountability. A Group Organization Management study underscores the efficacy of this approach, pointing to how a strategic rearticulation of innovative concepts can increase their palatability and perceived value among decision-makers who are predisposed to uphold the status quo.[67]

Such linguistic alchemy requires a thorough understanding of the bureaucratic mindset. Innovators must immerse themselves in the policy documents, strategic plans, and historical data that shape the institution's worldview. They must know how decisions are made, what metrics are valued, and the language that permeates the highest levels of the bureaucracy. With this knowledge, they can frame their innovations not as disruptions, but as enhancements or logical extensions of current practices.

For instance, when proposing a new digital platform, an innovator might emphasize how it aligns with governmental digital transformation goals, enhances data security (speaking to compliance), or streamlines service delivery (addressing efficiency). They might underscore the platform's ability to generate data analytics that support evidence-based policymaking, a key organizational goal for many public institutions.

By mastering the language of bureaucracy, innovators transform their role from that of outsiders trying to break in, to insiders pushing for progress. They become bilingual—fluent in both the language of innovation and the dialect of bureaucracy—and thus can act as translators, bridging the gap between what is and what could be. In doing so, they ensure that their innovative ideas gain the traction and support necessary to move from concept to reality within the conservative fabric of government institutions.

Small Wins Strategy: The 'Small Wins Strategy' is a judicious approach to innovation, especially within the meticulous and cautious domain of government bureaucracy. It advocates for starting with modest, manageable projects that can quickly demonstrate their worth and gather support before attempting to tackle more significant, systemic changes. This methodology is grounded in the principle that small successes can build momentum, establish a track record of effectiveness, and generate a cascading series of improvements that reshape the organizational culture towards embracing change.

In the context of government work, where every new initiative is scrutinized for its feasibility and cost-effectiveness, starting small is a strategic method to bypass the daunting wall of collective skepticism. It allows innovators to prove the concept of their ideas without over-committing resources. Small-scale projects can serve as pilots or prototypes, offering tangible evidence of their impact, which in turn can be used to persuade and win over stakeholders.

For example, an innovator looking to implement a new technology platform might begin by introducing it to a single department or team. This pilot project, small in scope, allows for a controlled testing environment to track outcomes, adjust for issues, and optimize processes without the pressure of a full-scale roll-out. As this small project succeeds, it serves as a proof of concept, demonstrating effectiveness and mitigating perceived risk.

These small wins are also significant for their psychological impact within the organization. They can ignite enthusiasm and confidence, making the idea of change less intimidating. Each success story becomes a narrative tool, showcasing the innovator's ability to deliver results and building their reputation as a catalyst for positive change.

Moreover, these incremental changes create a sense of progress and forward motion, which can be highly motivating for all involved. They generate data and insights that can inform future projects, creating a feedback loop that refines the innovation process. When these small projects align with broader strategic goals, they can act as stepping stones towards more ambitious endeavors, laying the groundwork for larger, transformative projects.

In essence, the Small Wins Strategy is about planting seeds of change and nurturing them with patience and precision. By demonstrating the art of the possible, one small win at a time, innovators can accumulate the social capital, empirical evidence, and organizational buy-in necessary to catalyze lasting change. In a risk-averse environment, this strategy becomes an innovator's chess game, where each calculated move builds towards an endgame of comprehensive, system-wide innovation.

Leveraging Data for Persuasion: The art of persuasion in the bureaucratic arena often hinges on the concrete and demonstrable. Herein lies the paramount role of data, serving as a critical tool in the innovator's arsenal. In the landscape of government decision-making, where evidence dictates direction, leveraging data is tantamount to speaking the most persuasive language of all: the language of indisputable facts and figures.

Data-driven proposals offer a clear narrative that can cut through the noise of competing priorities and entrenched habits. They offer measurable indicators of potential success, mitigating the perceived risks associated with new initiatives. By presenting data, innovators effectively communicate that their ideas are not rooted in mere speculation but are the culmination of rigorous analysis and strategic forecasting.

For instance, when proposing a new public service initiative, providing data on how similar programs have led to cost savings, increased public satisfaction, or improved operational efficiencies elsewhere can be compelling. This evidence-based approach can shift the conversation from one of uncertainty to one of informed opportunity. It demonstrates due diligence, showing that the innovator has not only envisioned a new idea but has also considered the empirical outcomes and implications.

Furthermore, leveraging data allows innovators to tailor their proposals to the specific values and objectives of their organization. It enables them to align their innovative concepts with the institution's mission, showing how the new ideas can quantitatively contribute to organizational goals. For example, if a government entity prioritizes sustainability, data illustrating how the proposed innovation can reduce carbon footprint can be a decisive factor in securing support.

Data also facilitates the setting of benchmarks and metrics for success, which are essential for tracking the progress and impact of the innovation post-implementation. This creates a feedback loop, where data not only justifies the initial adoption of the innovation but also continues to inform its development and scaling.

In essence, data is more than a mere instrument for persuasion; it is a cornerstone of credibility. It empowers innovators to build compelling cases that stand up to the scrutiny of the most critical stakeholders. In the meticulous and often conservative domain of public administration, where evidence is the currency of trust, leveraging data for persuasion is not just a strategy—it is a necessity for those seeking to introduce meaningful and transformative change.

Employing Patience and Persistence: The path of a public sector innovator is often a testament to endurance. The bureaucratic landscape can test one's resolve with its propensity for gradual pace and its penchant for the status quo. It is in this setting that patience and persistence emerge as vital virtues for the agent of change. The chronicles of public administration are replete with initiatives that, thanks to the unwavering commitment of their champions, have evolved from fledgling concepts to fixtures of government function.

Patience in this context is not passive waiting but rather an active stance of preparation and continuous improvement. It involves consistently advocating for the innovative vision, refining it, and remaining alert for opportunities to advance the cause. Persistence, on the other hand, manifests in the innovator's refusal to be daunted by setbacks. It is the resilience to push forth, to navigate the maze of administrative processes and policy considerations, and to sustain the momentum of the innovation through its various stages of maturity.

The longitudinal impact of such persistence is often remarkable. Initiatives that persevere through initial reluctance or outright resistance can become deeply embedded within the public service delivery framework, leading to reforms that outlast their creators. For example, many digital transformation projects in government, now seen as indispensable, were once considered optional or supplementary. It was the doggedness of forward-thinking individuals that saw such projects through the pilot stages, evaluation, and eventual adoption on a broad scale.

Real-world narratives abound with instances where a combination of patience and persistence proved to be the inflection point for institutional change. The tale of the telehealth champion is one of incremental advocacy, where each small pilot and each successful test case built upon the last, slowly but surely shifting the opinion of policymakers and stakeholders. Similarly, the environmental advocate's journey within municipal waste management demonstrates the power of steadfast commitment. Each successful composting cycle, each reduction in landfill use, each favorable report card on greenhouse gas emissions added weight to the argument for program expansion.

In these scenarios, the innovator's patience and persistence are underpinned by strategic navigation of the bureaucratic environment. They show an acute awareness of timing, an understanding of the ebb and flow of policy windows, and a capability to act decisively when the opportunity arises. The cultivation of allies, the adept framing of the innovation narrative, the incremental demonstration of benefits, and the strategic use of data all contribute to this delicate dance of patience and persistence.

Ultimately, these qualities are not just beneficial but essential for those looking to pioneer lasting change within the public sector. They define not only the journey but also the legacy of the public sector innovator. Through the lens of patience and persistence, what begins as a mere spark of an idea has the potential to illuminate the future of government service delivery, transforming systems and serving as a beacon for the next generation of innovators.

Each narrative underscores a powerful theme: conviction, when coupled with strategic insight and unwavering dedication, can triumph over the most entangling bureaucratic hurdles. These vignettes are not mere anecdotes; they are beacons, guiding the way for future innovators. They stand testament to the possibility of marrying personal conviction with professional duty to instigate meaningful, lasting change.

The innovator's dilemma is not an insurmountable impasse but a challenge to be met with a melding of strategic acumen and personal resolve. It is an invitation to navigate the complex dance of bureaucratic governance with finesse, wielding the tools of patience, persistence, and partnership. For those who rise to meet this challenge, the rewards extend beyond personal accomplishment; they contribute to the evolution of government, rendering it more dynamic, more responsive, and ultimately more attuned to the needs of the public it serves. The dance between innovation and bureaucracy thus continues, and the music plays on for those with the courage to step onto the floor.

6.2. Personal Triumphs: Government Employees Who Pioneered Change

In the vast ecosystem of government agencies, where protocols and procedures often eclipse the drive for innovation, Jane's solitary quest to overhaul the EPA's outdated paper-reliant system represents a beacon of progressive thought.[68] This narrative unfolds with Jane, a mid-level analyst whose passion for environmental preservation transcended her daily responsibilities. Observing mounds of paper waste generated by the EPA—an institution tasked with environmental protection—struck a dissonant chord with her professional ethos. The contradiction between the agency's core mission and its operations was stark, and Jane saw an opportunity not just for improvement but for revolution within the very fabric of the organization.[69]

Undeterred by the magnitude of her challenge, Jane meticulously gathered evidence of the inefficiencies and environmental detriments perpetuated by the agency's paper dependence. She foresaw a future where digital records could streamline processes, diminish environmental harm, and even fortify data security. With unyielding tenacity, Jane crafted a strategic proposal that addressed potential objections with clear, calculated answers. Her proposal didn't simply highlight the problems of the present; it painted a vivid portrait of a more efficient, eco-conscious, and technologically advanced future for the EPA.

Commencing her project on a modest scale, Jane launched a pilot within her own division, targeting a selection of processes to transition to digital platforms. The benefits became quickly apparent: documents were easier to search, information retrieval times plummeted, and the physical space once overwhelmed by file cabinets now stood repurposed for more productive use. This tangible success served as irrefutable evidence, turning initial skepticism among her peers into endorsements for the digital approach. Jane's initiative was transforming not only practices but also attitudes, recalibrating her colleagues' expectations of what constituted normal operations within the agency.

Jane's pilot project, marked by its success, garnered attention and support, allowing her to propel the digitization initiative forward. Her unwavering commitment acted as a gravitational force, pulling in other departments and decision-makers. Through cross-departmental collaborations, she expanded the project, drawing on the expertise of IT professionals and engaging in discussions with policy developers to ensure the scalability of her digitization project. This cross-pollination of ideas enriched the initiative, preparing it for expansion beyond the confines of a single department and into the broader institution.

The ripple effect of Jane's project was far-reaching; as digital records became the new standard within the EPA, this practice was soon championed as a model for other governmental bodies. National guidelines for digital record-keeping took shape, drawing from the framework and success metrics of Jane's initiative. The environmental benefits were quantifiable and significant, with the EPA setting a precedent for sustainable practices, encouraging other agencies to follow suit. The operational enhancements, in terms of both efficiency and security, signaled a modernization of governmental operations, showcasing the potential within these age-old institutions for meaningful and progressive change.

Jane's journey within the EPA is more than a story of personal success; it is an emblematic case study of how resilience, foresight, and strategic planning can converge to effect systemic change. She navigated the complex maze of bureaucracy with a singular focus, identifying and seizing an opportunity for improvement that aligned with the core values of environmental stewardship. Jane's experience lays out a clear trajectory for change:

- **Problem Identification:** She noticed the discrepancy between the EPA's mandate for environmental protection and its daily practices, sparking the initial idea for her initiative.
- **Visionary Thinking:** Jane had the insight to recognize that a digital transformation could serve as a lighthouse, guiding the agency toward a future aligned with its mission.
- **Resilience**: Even when faced with opposition and doubt, Jane used each challenge as an impetus to evolve her strategy and solidify her determination.
- **Cross-Pollination of Ideas**: She actively sought the perspectives of a diverse group of stakeholders to enrich the initiative, ensuring it was robust and comprehensive.
- **Scalability:** Understanding the need for proof of concept, Jane focused on the success of a smaller project before advocating for widespread implementation.

Jane's story serves as a clarion call to other public servants: innovation within government is not only possible but also necessary and achievable. Her story acts as an instructional tale for aspiring change-makers in the public sector, emphasizing that impactful transformation can arise from any tier of the organizational hierarchy. By chronicling her path, we uncover a blueprint for enacting change, demonstrating that the spirit of innovation can indeed penetrate and flourish within the structured and often rigid corridors of government bureaucracy.

6.3. Tools for the Innovative Spirit in a Conventional System

Innovation within the confines of a conventional system is akin to planting a garden in rocky soil. It requires not just the seeds of new ideas but also the cultivation techniques that can allow those ideas to take root and flourish despite the hard ground. The innovative spirit is the gardener's intuition, a blend of creativity, tenacity, and strategic thinking that respects the intricate ecosystem of the existing garden but is not limited by its current design. It is this spirit that must be harnessed and nurtured to transform the landscape of public service, blending the conventional with the novel, allowing them to coexist and coevolve.

As previously said, bureaucratic jargon and procedures, often seen as barriers, are in fact the keys to transformation. To innovate effectively, one must first become fluent in this language. Mastering the language of bureaucracy – from policy documents to legislative briefs – is akin to a musician learning scales; it is the foundational work that allows for improvisation and composition later on. A deep dive into the language of regulations can unveil hidden flexibilities, transforming a "no" into a "not yet," and, with persistence, into a "how." It's about perceiving the underlying principles that guide the rules and using that knowledge to navigate and, where possible, reshape them. For example, understanding the intent behind compliance can lead to creating solutions that meet both the letter and the spirit of regulations, thus opening avenues for innovation that were previously concealed by a superficial reading.

Navigating the Hierarchy with Emotional Intelligence: Emotional intelligence is the compass that guides one through the often-uncharted waters of bureaucratic hierarchies. It is the ability to read the undercurrents of organizational charts, to recognize the human element in the most mechanical of systems. This skill enables the building of relationships that transcend the rigid formalities of rank and file. Allies and champions for innovation are found through an understanding of others' motivations, fears, and aspirations. By leveraging emotional intelligence, one can craft proposals that speak to these motivations, aligning innovative ideas with the personal and professional goals of decision-makers within the system.

The Power of Data: In the realm of government, data is the bedrock upon which sound decisions are built. It gives substance to new ideas, grounding them in reality and providing the evidence needed to challenge the inertia of established ways. Data analytics can be employed to uncover inefficiencies, forecast outcomes, and substantiate the impact of innovative proposals. Nevertheless, it's crucial not to overlook the power of qualitative data. Stories and testimonials imbue numbers with meaning, transforming them from abstract figures into narratives of real-world impact. These stories can sway opinions, ignite passions, and spur action in ways that raw data alone cannot.

Leveraging Technology for Incremental Change: Not all innovation must be disruptive. Many times, the most significant transformations result from a series of small, strategic changes. Technology can be a formidable ally in this gradual process. The introduction of a new software that streamlines document processing can reclaim countless hours for creative thought and strategic planning. Simple tools, such as collaborative platforms, can dismantle silos, fostering an environment ripe for cross-departmental innovation and shared vision.

Prototyping and Pilot Programs: Pilot programs serve as the proving grounds for the public sector, offering a miniature model of how broader systems could operate under innovative changes. Starting with a small-scale model allows for the demonstration of an idea's viability, refinement through real-world application, and ultimately, a persuasive case for its broader adoption. Prototyping—be it a process or a digital tool—invites iterative development and feedback, which are essential in environments where risk is typically avoided. These microcosms of innovation can become powerful examples, illustrating the benefits of change without necessitating widespread upheaval.

Mentorship and Networking: The fusion of experience and innovation can lead to profound growth and change within bureaucratic systems. Mentorship programs pair the visionaries with the veterans, combining the boldness of new perspectives with the wisdom of navigated paths. Networking extends beyond immediate departments, fostering a broader understanding of systemic challenges and opportunities for innovation. These connections are the conduits through which ideas flow, blending the insights of one department with the needs of another, creating a fertile ground for shared innovation.

Advocacy and Policy Engagement: A nuanced understanding of the legislative process is indispensable for enacting change. Advocacy tools, such as drafting policy papers or engaging in public consultations, enable one to participate actively in shaping the conversation around new policies. Mastery of policy engagement allows public servants to assert their voice in the development of new initiatives, advocating for innovation before it becomes a necessity.

Resilience and Self-Care: Innovation is an endurance race, demanding not just intellectual rigor but also emotional stamina. The resilience to persist in the face of setbacks is as much a tool as any technological innovation or policy proposal. Practices of self-care and mindfulness, along with support from professional networks, ensure that one's mental and emotional wellsprings are continually replenished. It is only by maintaining this personal equilibrium that one can sustain the prolonged effort needed to implement transformative change.

These tools constitute a kit for nurturing the innovative spirit within the conventional system. They are not comprehensive but serve as a solid starting point for those looking to make a difference. Each tool must be employed with deliberation, empathy, and a forward-looking vision. Supported by this toolkit, the innovative spirit can indeed find fertile ground in even the most traditional of systems, cultivating change that is both profound and lasting.

CHAPTER 7

The Ethical Compass: Navigating Moral Dilemmas

7.1. When Rules Conflict with Conscience

In the heart of governance, the interplay of laws and regulations is a tableau on which public servants paint the portrait of society. They hold the brushes of power and responsibility, yet the palette is not theirs alone—it's a shared spectrum of the public's values, ethics, and conscience. Each stroke is a decision, each hue a choice that reflects the complex relationship between the rigidity of rules and the flexibility of personal conscience. The navigation through this space is an art form requiring a deep understanding of the rules and a profound engagement with one's ethical beliefs.

Imagine the corridors of power where public servants move like silent sentinels of society's conscience. Here, the established rules form the architecture within which they operate, but the pillars of personal moral beliefs are what truly support their resolve. When these rules seem to contradict one's moral compass, the issue transcends mere compliance; it becomes a profound dialogue on reconciling the duties of one's role with the call of one's ethical convictions. For a public servant, these conflicts are not hypothetical musings of ethics classes—they are palpable, real-life scenarios that play out in the decisions impacting lives and communities.

Consider a policy crafted with the intent to streamline urban development by relocating underprivileged communities. The policy's text is unambiguous, the expected outcomes clear, but through the lens of personal conscience, the shades of injustice and displacement are unmistakable. Such policies, when viewed through a personal ethical lens, reveal the stark contrasts between the black-and-white nature of rules and the rich spectrum of personal ethics.

Herein lies the essence of ethical decision-making in public service. It is not a mechanical process of ticking boxes or a cold calculation of pros and cons. It is a deeply human process that involves a thoughtful examination of one's values, the courage to question, and the wisdom to discern the most ethically sound path. It is about understanding the layers of implications that each choice unfurls, the ripples each decision sends across the societal pond.

Engaging with ethical frameworks is an integral part of this discernment process. These frameworks offer not just a theoretical underpinning for decision-making but serve as beacons guiding public servants through the murky waters of ethical dilemmas. They empower public servants to parse through the dimensions of their conflicts, weigh the outcomes of their actions, and reflect deeply on the kind of professionals they aspire to be—ones who lead not only with their minds but with their hearts as well.

Ethical pluralism acknowledges the rich tapestry of moral beliefs that public servants bring to the table. It fosters an environment where diverse ethical viewpoints are not just tolerated but engaged with earnestly—a dialogue that seeks not to homogenize but to harmonize differing ethical stances. This pluralism is the bedrock of a democratic society, and engaging with it allows for a deeper understanding that one's personal ethical stance is part of a grander conversation about values, justice, and the collective good.

When rules and conscience stand in opposition, the path forward is not about choosing one over the other, but rather about seeking a harmonious balance that honors both. This balance may involve negotiating within the system to enact change, championing policy reform, or finding innovative applications of the rules that alleviate ethical concerns. It is a balance that demands not only intellectual rigor but also emotional intelligence and a deep sense of empathy.

Into this complex arena, we introduce the narrative of Nora, whose story is etched in the annals of a bustling city housing department. It's a narrative that unfolds amidst the familiar office symphony—the aromatic allure of coffee, the rhythmic hum of machinery, and the soft cadence of keystrokes. In this setting, Nora's role as a mid-level manager often positioned her at the confluence of policy and humanity, where the abstract became tangible with every form filled, every decision stamped.

Nora's daily encounters with the city's marginalized—a tableau of the homeless, the impoverished, and the displaced—grounded her belief in the transformative power of her work. To her, providing housing was not just a matter of allocating resources but a sacred duty to bestow dignity and hope. Yet, on an autumn morning that dawned like any other, Nora found herself at a crossroads when a policy aimed at "cleaning up" the city's image threatened to unravel the fabric of the community she served.

The directive was clear: remove the homeless from public spaces to rejuvenate the city's core. It was a policy lauded by many, a beacon of urban renewal, but it also cast a long shadow—one that would displace hundreds without a promise of sanctuary or solace. Nora grappled with the rationale behind the directive, her conscience rebelling against the human toll it exacted.

Nora's response to this ethical conundrum was not one of defiance but one of steadfast determination. She shouldered the dilemma with a profound sense of responsibility, fully aware that the easier path would be to acquiesce to the demands of the directive, to become an unresisting component in the bureaucratic apparatus. Yet, guided by a moral compass attuned to the frequencies of compassion and empathy, Nora recognized that inaction was a luxury she could not afford, both professionally and personally.

In her quest for a resolution, Nora turned to the very people whose lives hung in the balance. She collected their stories—tales etched with the struggle for survival under the open sky, statistics that bore the mark of human existence. With this compendium of lived experiences, Nora approached her superiors not with antagonism but with an appeal to the shared values of humanity and social responsibility. She advocated for an approach that reconciled the city's aspirations for renewal with the imperative of compassion.

Nora's advocacy did not revolutionize the policy with the stroke of a pen, but it ignited a spark of dialogue. Her department began to entertain the notion of integrating social workers into their processes, of viewing the homeless not as a blight to be eradicated but as members of the community deserving of aid and respect. Nora's narrative evolved into a quiet yet potent force of influence, a testament to the enduring power of ethical conviction amidst professional obligations.

Nora's journey is emblematic of the countless public servants who navigate the intricate dance between rules and conscience every day. Her story serves as a poignant reminder that the mechanisms of governance, as formidable and rigid as they may appear, are ultimately human constructs—endowed with humanity through the conscientious actions of those who operate within their bounds. Nora's tale is more than a solitary account of ethical fortitude; it is a beacon of potential systemic transformation, an affirmation that each decision, made with thoughtful consideration and compassionate intent, contributes to the larger mosaic of governance.

The lessons gleaned from historical and contemporary narratives of ethical dilemmas are invaluable, offering both cautionary tales and wellsprings of inspiration. They underscore the enduring nature of the conflict between rules and conscience and highlight the opportunity to engage with these complexities in ways that are both constructive and meaningful. These stories remind us that the tension between policy and personal ethics is not a battleground but a fertile ground for growth and ethical maturation.

Ultimately, ethical decision-making in public service is about aligning one's actions with the timeless principles of integrity, fairness, and respect for the intrinsic worth of every individual. It involves a conscious awareness of the impact of those actions and a commitment to continuous learning and personal growth. It is a journey that intertwines the personal with the professional, challenging public servants to serve not merely as functionaries but as exemplars of justice and ethical stewardship in their pursuit of a society that is equitable, just, and humane.

7.2. Integrity in the Shadows: Dealing with Ethical Grey Areas

In the nuanced world of governance, the realm of ethical ambiguity exists far from the safety of clear statutes and the firm ground of regulations. Here, in the uncertain domain where policy is silent, public servants find themselves navigating the challenging terrain of ethical grey areas. These are the junctures where rules fade into the background, and the internal compass of morality must guide decision-making. It's a place where the abstract notion of 'right' and 'wrong' is not easily parsed by the written law but instead resides in the complex interplay of ethical nuances that each unique situation presents.

Ella, a seasoned city planner in a large and ever-evolving metropolis, knew this realm all too well. Her daily responsibilities carried the weight of decisions that would shape the city's future. She worked within a framework of policies that were designed to ensure the well-being and growth of the city. Yet, there were moments when these guidelines provided no sanctuary for her conscience, moments when the policies that dictated action fell short of addressing the nuanced realities of urban life. Ella found herself in these ethical grey areas more often than she had anticipated, each time facing the challenge of aligning her professional duties with her personal ethical standards.

It was during the orchestration of a major urban development project that Ella encountered a poignant ethical dilemma. The project was ambitious and held the promise of rejuvenating a neglected quarter of the city. It was poised to inject new life into an area marred by time, to erect modernity where there was decay. The blueprint was clear in its objectives, but hidden among the lines of potential and progress was a detail that troubled Ella deeply. A small community garden, cultivated lovingly by local residents over many years, was to be uprooted.

To the developers, it was a negligible sacrifice for the greater good. To Ella, and to those who found solace in its green embrace, it was a symbol of community and history—a fragment of nature where urban residents connected not just with the earth but with each other.

The policy directives were unambiguous in prioritizing economic development over such a small-scale community project. Yet, Ella understood that the garden represented something invaluable that couldn't be quantified or replaced by modern structures. It wasn't just about the loss of a green space; it was about the erosion of community identity and the disregard for the environment that played a vital role in the neighborhood's fabric. The decision she faced was emblematic of the conflicts that often arise in public service—conflicts between the advancement of the city and the preservation of its soul.

Choosing not to resign herself to the path of least resistance, Ella sought a resolution that would honor both the project's ambitions and the community's attachment to the garden. She initiated a series of dialogues with the stakeholders, approaching each discussion not as a formality but as an essential platform for understanding and collaboration. Ella listened to the residents' stories of what the garden meant to them, their narratives weaving a tapestry of memories and meaning that the garden held.

Through these conversations, a new vision for the development project began to take shape—one that integrated the existing greenery with the new infrastructure. It was a vision that required Ella to advocate tirelessly, challenging her superiors to expand their definition of development to include social and environmental considerations. She compiled data on the psychological and health benefits of communal green spaces, reinforcing her argument with evidence of their value.

The final design was a tribute to Ella's conviction and her ability to harmonize different priorities. It included pockets of green woven into the new development, ensuring that the essence of the community garden lived on, albeit in a new form. This outcome was not just a victory for the neighborhood but a landmark in Ella's career. It stood as proof that even without explicit guidelines, innovative and ethically sound solutions were achievable.

Ella's experience is a powerful testament to the role of integrity in public service, especially when navigating the grey areas of governance. Her story demonstrates that it is possible to find equilibrium—a place where the call of duty does not silence the whisper of conscience. It's a delicate balance, attained not by surrendering to one side but by engaging in a thoughtful quest for solutions that serve the greater good without forsaking core values.

In public service, Ella's story is not an anomaly but a reflection of the many unseen battles fought in the name of integrity. Across departments and agencies, there are countless individuals like Ella who operate within these grey zones, making decisions that never make headlines but shape the lives of people in profound ways. They are the unsung heroes, the custodians of trust, whose every decision is a reaffirmation of their unwavering commitment to ethical service.

In the absence of black-and-white guidelines, these public servants demonstrate that integrity and humanity can, and indeed must, extend beyond the written rulebook. Their dedication ensures that even in the most ambiguous of circumstances, the spirit of public service is upheld. Their stories, while often untold, are a powerful reminder that in the realm of governance, integrity is the light that guides through the shadows of ethical uncertainty.

7.3. Profiles in Courage: Individuals Who Upheld Integrity Over Expediency

In the vast and often faceless expanse of public service, there are those who become beacons of moral guidance, not through the clamor of grand achievements, but through the quiet resolve of their ethical convictions. Their deeds form the very bedrock of courage in the face of moral dilemmas, standing as testament to the unwavering strength that upholds integrity over the siren call of expediency. This section is dedicated to those stalwart souls whose legacies are etched deep in the annals of bureaucratic lore, serving as profound lessons in the art of ethical decision-making within the complex web of governance.

These individuals are the exemplars who navigate the nuanced corridors of power and policy with an inner compass calibrated to the true north of ethical conduct. They embody the courage that comes not from a blind adherence to procedure but from a readiness to place integrity at the forefront of their actions. Their narratives offer rich insights into the moral fortitude required to prioritize ethical integrity over the allure of quick fixes in the intricate dance of governance.

When integrity in the public sphere is invoked, it often conjures images of high profile acts of defiance against systemic injustices. However, true ethical courage often reveals itself in the more subdued, yet equally profound, moments—decisions made under the soft glow of a desk lamp, quiet refusals to ride the wave of convenience, and the steadfast commitment to honor the public trust, even when accolades are absent.

Through the narratives of these steadfast individuals—their challenges, their dilemmas, and the profound wisdom distilled from their experiences—we gain a window into the soul of public service marked by integrity.

The Whistleblower's Dilemma: In the labyrinthine corridors of the financial regulatory agency, Michael, a seasoned analyst, navigated the complex world of fiscal oversight with a keen eye and an unwavering commitment to the public good. His days were often a blend of meticulous data analysis and intricate policy reviews, a routine that demanded precision and ethical vigilance.

Michael's journey into the heart of an ethical storm began on an unassuming spring morning. While reviewing a series of routine financial reports, he stumbled upon irregularities that set off alarm bells. These were not mere clerical errors but pointed to a systemic oversight that allowed significant regulatory violations to slip through the cracks. The implications were grave—unchecked, these lapses could lead to consumer fraud on a massive scale, eroding public trust and inflicting untold financial damage on the unsuspecting populace.

As Michael delved deeper, the magnitude of the issue became starkly apparent. What he uncovered was a network of loopholes and neglected checks, a pattern of negligence that extended far beyond what he had initially suspected. The convenient path would have been to gloss over these findings, to file them away as anomalies. After all, bringing them to light would mean stepping into a whirlwind of controversy, challenging powerful figures within the agency, and potentially inciting public uproar.

But Michael, guided by a steadfast belief in the sanctity of his duty, chose to stand in the line of fire. His decision was not made in haste. Nights of introspection and moral reckoning followed, where the weight of potential consequences loomed large. Conversations with his family underscored the personal risks involved—professional alienation, scrutiny under the public eye, and the daunting prospect of becoming a pariah in his field.

Despite these foreboding clouds, Michael's resolve solidified. Armed with extensive documentation and an unshakeable sense of purpose, he took the step of blowing the whistle on the agency's failings. The fallout was immediate and turbulent. Michael found himself at the epicenter of an institutional storm—facing scrutiny from his superiors, skepticism from some colleagues, and a barrage of legal and procedural challenges.

But his revelations set in motion a series of events that would fundamentally transform the agency's operations. Investigations were launched, leading to the overhaul of regulatory practices and the implementation of stringent checks that plugged the loopholes Michael had exposed. His actions reverberated beyond the walls of his agency, prompting a broader discourse on accountability and transparency in financial governance.

Michael's journey was fraught with personal challenges. He faced moments of doubt and isolation, times when the burden of his choice weighed heavily on his shoulders. Yet, amidst these trials, there emerged a story of unwavering courage—a narrative that resonated with others in the agency who had silently acknowledged the system's flaws but felt powerless to act.

In the aftermath, Michael's role as a whistleblower was not just about exposing malpractices. It became a beacon that illuminated the importance of ethical resilience in public service. His story inspired a cultural shift within the agency, nurturing an environment where integrity was valued and encouraged.

Today, Michael's tale is shared among his peers and newcomers as a lesson in moral bravery. His experience has become a part of the agency's ethos, a reminder of the vigilance required to safeguard the public trust. It stands as a testament to the impact one individual can have in steering an institution back to its foundational principles of honesty and accountability.

Michael's narrative, woven with threads of integrity and courage, serves as a potent reminder of the power of truth. It underscores the pivotal role of individuals in upholding the tenets of transparency and accountability, particularly in the realms where public welfare is at stake. His story is not just a chronicle of personal valor but a blueprint for ethical stewardship in public service—a clarion call to all who bear the mantle of public trust.

The Advocate for Equity: Sarah's journey as a public health official was marked by an unwavering commitment to bridging the healthcare divide. Her story began in the bustling corridors of the health department, where she worked amidst a maze of statistics and policy documents. It was in this environment, often detached from the realities of the very people it aimed to serve, that Sarah discovered her true calling.

Her awakening to the disparities in healthcare access came gradually, through interactions with community leaders, patient testimonials, and a deep analysis of health outcome data. She noticed a distressing pattern: minority communities were consistently receiving substandard healthcare due to a combination of systemic barriers and overlooked needs. This revelation was more than a professional concern for Sarah; it struck a chord with her personal values of justice and equality.

Driven by a sense of duty that transcended her job description,

Sarah embarked on a mission to dismantle these barriers. She started by meticulously gathering data, pouring over health statistics, and patient access reports. Her findings painted a stark picture of inequity: longer wait times for appointments in minority neighborhoods, a lack of culturally competent healthcare providers, and a dearth of resources in languages other than English.

Equipped with this data, Sarah began her advocacy, first within the walls of her department. She organized presentations for her colleagues and superiors, highlighting the inequities and proposing policy changes. While her initial efforts were met with bureaucratic hesitation, Sarah was undeterred. She understood that change in such a large institution would require persistence and a broader coalition of support.

Sarah reached out to community organizations, healthcare professionals, and patient advocacy groups, sharing her findings and rallying them around the cause of equitable healthcare. She organized community forums, inviting residents to share their experiences and concerns. These forums were eye-opening for many of her colleagues, who had been unaware of the extent of the disparities. The stories shared at these events were powerful and humanizing, transforming abstract data into compelling narratives of struggle and resilience.

As her network of allies grew, so did the momentum for change. Sarah and her coalition began to push for policy reforms, advocating for the allocation of more resources to underserved areas, the recruitment of healthcare providers from diverse backgrounds, and the development of culturally sensitive health education materials.

The road to reform was fraught with challenges. There were budget constraints, political pushbacks, and a deeply entrenched resistance to change. But Sarah's unwavering commitment and the growing support from the community and her allies within the department gradually turned the tide.

The culmination of her efforts was the implementation of a series of reforms that fundamentally transformed the department's approach to healthcare. New clinics were opened in underserved neighborhoods, staffed by professionals trained in cultural competency. Health education materials were translated into multiple languages, and community health programs were established, focusing on preventive care and awareness.

Sarah's legacy in the department is more than just the policies she helped change; it is the shift in mindset she catalyzed. She instilled a sense of responsibility towards equity and inclusivity, principles that are now ingrained in the department's mission. Her journey serves as a powerful testament to the impact one individual can have in championing systemic change.

Today, Sarah continues her advocacy, her voice a constant in the ongoing conversation about healthcare equity. Her story is a beacon of hope and a reminder that in the quest for a fairer and more just society, perseverance, data-driven advocacy, and coalition-building are formidable tools. Her narrative is not just a chapter in the annals of public health policy but a roadmap for all who aspire to make a difference in their communities.

The Ethical Negotiator: In the intricate world of international trade negotiations, Emma stood out not just for her astute diplomatic skills, but for her unwavering ethical compass. As a seasoned diplomat, she was well-acquainted with the delicate balancing act of advancing her country's interests while navigating the complex tapestry of international relations. Her career, a mosaic of delicate negotiations and strategic alliances, was marked by a profound commitment to ethical integrity.

Emma's defining moment came during a high-stakes trade negotiation involving multiple countries. The discussions promised significant economic benefits for her nation, but they were mired in controversy over labor practices in some of the participating countries. Reports of labor rights violations, including unsafe working conditions and child labor, cast a long shadow over the proceedings.

For many, the lure of economic gains might have overshadowed these ethical concerns, but for Emma, they were central to the integrity of the agreement. She believed passionately that trade should not come at the cost of human dignity and that her country had a responsibility to set a higher standard in international commerce.

Emma embarked on a mission to infuse the trade agreement with strong labor protections. She started by meticulously gathering evidence of the violations, collaborating with NGOs, labor unions, and human rights advocates. She compiled reports, firsthand accounts, and statistical data that painted a harrowing picture of the human toll behind the proposed trade benefits.

Armed with this evidence, Emma faced a formidable challenge in the negotiation rooms. She encountered resistance, not only from the countries accused of labor violations but also from some of her own colleagues and superiors who were wary of jeopardizing the economic benefits of the deal. Emma, however, stood her ground, articulating her case with a blend of moral clarity and diplomatic acumen.

In a series of intense negotiations, she worked tirelessly to bring her counterparts on board. She proposed the inclusion of a labor chapter in the agreement, outlining strict standards for worker safety, fair wages, and the prohibition of child labor. She argued that these measures were not only moral imperatives but would also create a level playing field for all countries involved.

Emma's advocacy extended beyond the negotiation table. She engaged with the media, participated in public forums, and liaised with lawmakers, building a groundswell of support for her stance. She highlighted how the agreement, with robust labor standards, could serve as a model for future trade deals, promoting sustainable and ethical trade practices globally.

After months of relentless efforts, Emma's persistence paid off. The final agreement included comprehensive labor protections, marking a significant milestone in international trade policy. Her role in shaping this agreement elevated her nation's standing as a champion of ethical trade practices.

Emma's story is a beacon of integrity in the often opaque world of international diplomacy. Her commitment to human rights and labor standards in the face of immense pressure is a testament to the impact that one individual can have in shaping global policies. She demonstrated that ethical considerations need not be casualties of economic pursuits but can be integral components of international agreements.

Today, Emma continues to be a respected figure in diplomatic circles, known for her principled approach and her ability to navigate complex ethical landscapes with grace and determination. Her legacy is not just in the policies she helped shape but in the broader message she imparted: that in the realm of global governance, ethical integrity and steadfast commitment to human dignity can and should drive the course of international relations.

Her narrative serves as a guiding light for current and future diplomats, showing that true success in diplomacy is measured not just by the agreements signed but by the values upheld. Emma's journey underscores the enduring importance of ethical leadership in public service, a reminder that integrity and a deep commitment to the public good should be at the heart of all diplomatic endeavors.

The integrity displayed by Michael, Sarah, and Emma—their choices and the paths they forged—constitute the moral sinew of public service. Their actions, characterized by a consistent dedication to ethical principles, teach us that integrity may often demand sacrifices, that the journey is fraught with challenges, but the destination fortifies the very foundations of trust upon which public institutions stand.

The profiles of these courageous individuals illuminate the ethical quandaries inherent in public service and serve as guiding lights through the murky waters of governance. They remind us that when confronted with the dichotomy of ease and righteousness, the path of integrity, though steeped in solitude and adversity, ultimately carves a legacy of trust and respect that endures the test of time.

Their accounts, rich in lessons and moral direction, offer us a compass by which to navigate our own ethical complexities, challenging us to reflect on how we might act when faced with similar crossroads. They inspire a commitment to uphold the noblest values of public service—integrity, fairness, and an unwavering dedication to the public good.

In the quiet shadows of bureaucracy, individuals these have upheld their ethical compasses, casting a light that illuminates the path for all who follow. Their legacy is a testament to the enduring power of integrity in governance, and their stories form a moral blueprint for current and future generations of public servants. Their tales are not inscribed for their own glorification but as enduring chapters in the narrative of ethical public service—a narrative that continues to evolve with each act of courage and each decision made in the sacred trust of the public.

CHAPTER 8

Carving a Path: Personal Growth in a Public Sector

8.1. The Narrative of Policy: Connecting People with Process

Policy-making, at its core, is about sculpting the contours of society, where abstract concepts and quantifiable data converge to shape real lives. This intersection is where the true power of policy lies—not in its technicalities, but in its potential to touch lives and transform communities. The narrative of policy, therefore, is not merely a sequence of legislative procedures but a tapestry woven from the diverse strands of individual experiences.

Incorporating personal stories into the policy-making framework brings a crucial dimension to this process. These narratives serve as a vivid reminder that behind every statistic, there is a human story. For instance, when formulating policies on housing, hearing from those who have grappled with homelessness offers invaluable insights that numbers alone cannot provide. Their experiences illuminate the daily realities of policy impacts, revealing nuances that might otherwise be overlooked in policy discussions.

Such narratives do more than just inform policy; they transform it. They breathe life into the skeletal structure of laws and regulations, infusing them with relevance and urgency. This transformation is particularly evident in areas like healthcare, where patient stories have profoundly shaped policies on mental health and chronic illness care. These narratives have a way of cutting through bureaucratic jargon, anchoring policy debates in the concrete experiences of those most affected.

Moreover, personal stories in policy-making enhance empathy, a critical yet often missing element in governmental decision-making. Empathy drives a deeper understanding of the issues at stake, urging policymakers to look beyond the confines of data and consider the human element of their decisions. This empathetic approach leads to policies that are not only more effective but also more equitable.

Additionally, personal narratives can significantly increase public engagement. When people see their own experiences, or those similar to theirs, reflected in policy discussions, they feel more connected to the process. This connection is crucial in building trust between the governed and the government, fostering a sense of shared responsibility and collective effort in addressing societal challenges.

In this reimagined view, policy-making becomes a process inherently connected to the people it serves, a blend of empirical analysis and empathetic storytelling. This approach fosters a governance model that is dynamic, inclusive, and deeply rooted in the fabric of human experience, ensuring that policies are not only crafted in the halls of power but also echo in the narratives of those who live under their influence. This perspective not only enhances the effectiveness of policies but also strengthens the democratic fabric by making governance more participatory and reflective of the diverse experiences within society.

Section Coaching:

Checklist for Incorporating the Narrative of Policy in Organizational Leadership

Identify Real Stories: Actively seek personal stories and experiences related to the policy issue. These stories should come from individuals directly affected by the policy.

Create Platforms for Sharing: Establish forums, surveys, or focus groups where people can share their experiences and insights. Ensure these platforms are accessible and inclusive.

Integrate Stories into Policy Analysis: Use personal narratives to complement quantitative data. Let these stories highlight the human impact of policy decisions.

Train Staff in Empathetic Listening: Equip your team with the skills to listen empathetically to stakeholders' stories. Understanding and acknowledging these narratives is crucial.

Prioritize Human-Centered Design in Policy Making: Design policies with a focus on the people they impact. Consider the human element in every aspect of policy development.

Use Narratives to Communicate Policy Goals: Incorporate personal stories in the communication of policy goals to the public. This approach makes policies more relatable and understandable.

Foster a Culture of Empathy: Encourage a workplace culture that values empathy and understanding, reflecting these values in policy-making processes.

Balance Data with Narratives: While data is crucial, balance it with personal stories to ensure policies address real-world complexities and human needs.

Encourage Transparency and Public Engagement: Be transparent about how personal narratives influence policy decisions. Engage the public regularly to build trust and participation.

Review and Adjust Policies Based on Feedback: Continuously review policies in light of new narratives and experiences, and be willing to adjust strategies as necessary.

Educate Policymakers on the Power of Stories: Train policymakers on the importance of narratives in understanding and shaping policies.

Document and Share Success Stories: Highlight cases where narratives have positively influenced policy decisions, sharing these stories both internally and publicly.

Ensure Ethical Use of Personal Stories: Respect privacy and consent when using personal narratives. Use stories ethically and responsibly.

Promote Inclusivity in Narrative Collection: Ensure that the collection of narratives represents diverse perspectives, especially from marginalized or underrepresented groups.

Evaluate the Impact of Narrative-Driven Policies: Regularly assess the effectiveness of policies that were influenced by personal stories to understand their impact and refine future approaches.

8.2. From Anecdotes to Action: Crafting Policy with Compassion

Policies, at their most transformative, emerge when they are woven from the threads of individual narratives. These stories, rich in personal experiences, are not just embellishments to the dry text of legislation; they are its essence, bringing a pulsating heartbeat to the otherwise static framework of governance. This chapter delves into the art of translating personal experiences into the language of policy, underscoring the potential of these narratives to shape, refine, and humanize the process of governance. Delving into individual narratives means engaging with the unique circumstances, hopes, and challenges of people from all walks of life. It's about understanding how a policy on paper translates into the daily reality of someone's life. A student struggling with loan debt, a senior citizen navigating the complexities of healthcare, or a family facing housing insecurity – each story provides invaluable context that can transform and enrich the policy-making process.

The power of personal stories in policy-making lies in their ability to transform abstract numbers and impersonal data into tangible human experiences. Imagine a policy shaped not just by statistical analysis but by the lived experiences of those it impacts. For instance, a teacher's tale from within the walls of an underfunded school, a narrative of a patient lost in the labyrinth of healthcare bureaucracy, or a small business owner's struggle against red tape. These stories, when interlaced with policy development, lend a depth of understanding that raw data alone cannot provide. The teacher's narrative could unveil the day-to-day challenges of delivering quality education in under-resourced settings, highlighting areas for targeted policy interventions. The patient's story might reveal systemic inefficiencies and bureaucratic hurdles in healthcare, guiding reforms for more patient-centric services. The small business owner's experiences could expose the practical impacts of regulatory complexities, paving the way for streamlined procedures.

Incorporating these narratives into policy-making requires a skillful balance. It's about empathetically listening to the real concerns and experiences of the people and translating these into actionable policy. This approach not only enhances the effectiveness of the policy but also ensures that it resonates more deeply with those it aims to serve. It's a step towards a governance that is not only for the people but also by the people, reflecting their diverse experiences and needs. Policymaking, in this sense, becomes a collaborative endeavor, a partnership between those who govern and those who are governed. It's an ongoing dialogue, where the voices of the community are not just heard but actively shape the outcome. This dynamic interaction ensures that policies are not just imposed but co-created, fostering a sense of ownership and alignment with the community's aspirations.

Crafting policy with this human-centric approach can lead to more innovative and effective solutions. Stories often highlight unmet needs and emerging challenges, inspiring creative solutions that might not emerge from traditional policy analysis. They challenge assumptions, encouraging policymakers to explore new avenues and think outside the conventional frameworks. For example, community stories might inspire innovative approaches to urban development that prioritize green spaces and public amenities, or they might lead to the adoption of alternative education models that better cater to diverse learning needs. By remaining open to the insights gleaned from personal experiences, policymakers can design more adaptable, forward-thinking policies that are better equipped to meet the evolving needs of society.

Yet, the incorporation of personal narratives into policy-making is not without challenges. It requires an ongoing commitment to keep these stories at the forefront, ensuring they are not overshadowed by political agendas or lost in bureaucratic processes. It involves continual engagement with communities, actively seeking out their stories and experiences, and weaving them into the fabric of policy decisions. This commitment extends beyond mere consultation; it's about building enduring relationships with communities, creating channels for continuous feedback, and ensuring that policies remain grounded in the lived realities of the people they affect. Policymakers need to cultivate an environment where these narratives are valued as critical inputs, fostering a culture of listening and learning within governmental institutions.

Crafting policy with compassion, grounded in the rich tapestry of personal stories, fosters a governance that is empathetic, responsive, and effective. It transforms the process of policy-making into an inclusive and democratic practice, enhancing the connection between the government and its citizens. This approach not only enriches the process of creating policy but also deepens the democratic fabric of society, ensuring that governance is reflective of the diverse experiences and aspirations of its people. A policy rooted in compassion and understanding is more likely to engender trust and cooperation from the public, creating a virtuous cycle where policies are not only well-received but also more effectively implemented.

Through this lens, policy-making transcends the realm of bureaucratic exercise and becomes a dynamic, inclusive process. It's a path that weaves together the empirical and the empathetic, creating policies that not only serve the populace but also resonate with their collective journey. This approach to governance is not just about serving the people; it's about understanding them, their stories, and their needs, and reflecting these in every policy crafted and implemented. In doing so, governance becomes more than a mere mechanism for organizing society; it becomes a platform for empowering it, for weaving the diverse threads of individual experiences into a cohesive and vibrant tapestry of communal life.

Section Coaching: Tips for Crafting Policy with Compassion

Facilitate Storytelling: Establish forums, town halls, and social platforms where individuals can share their experiences directly with policymakers.

Implement Ethnographic Research: Encourage policymakers to conduct fieldwork, immersing themselves in the communities they serve to understand the context behind the stories.

Practice Analytical Empathy: Train policymakers to not just listen to stories but to critically analyze them to identify systemic issues that policies can address.

Integrate Stories at Every Stage: Ensure that personal anecdotes are considered during policy conceptualization, drafting, and post-implementation feedback cycles.

Create Dedicated Roles: Set up departments or roles such as an 'Office of Public Engagement' focused on integrating personal narratives into policy-making.

Leverage Technology: Use digital platforms to collect and share personal stories widely, allowing for a broader range of voices to be heard.

Ensure Continuous Feedback: Develop a feedback loop where policies are regularly evaluated and adjusted based on new stories and data from the community.

Democratize the Process: Make policy drafts and discussions available and understandable to the public, inviting them to see how their stories shape government actions.

Foster Trust through Transparency: Be open about how stories have influenced policy decisions, highlighting specific narratives and the resulting changes.

Promote Policy as a Service: Frame policy-making as a service to the community, with the aim to address real-life challenges and improve daily lives.

8.3. Living Legislation: How Personal Experiences Shape Public Policy

The concept of living legislation emerges from the understanding that the most impactful laws and policies are those deeply rooted in the personal experiences and narratives of individuals. These are not abstract, faceless statutes but vibrant expressions of the collective human condition. This phenomenon, where the rich tapestry of personal stories is intricately woven into the fabric of policy-making, births legislation that pulsates with the realities of life. It is a transformative process that fundamentally shifts the essence of governance, making it more empathetic, relevant, and attuned to the people it is designed to serve.

The journey of a single story into the realm of policy-making can be a powerful catalyst for change. Consider the tale of a single mother balancing the demands of work and childcare, a narrative that echoes the struggles of countless others. Her experience, when voiced, highlights the challenges faced by working parents, prompting policymakers to consider more family-friendly employment laws or childcare support initiatives.

The story of Laura, a single mother from a small Midwestern town, encapsulates the struggles and resilience of millions of single parents across the nation. Laura worked as a receptionist at a local clinic, a job that barely paid enough to cover her living expenses and the needs of her six-year-old daughter, Emily. Her daily life was a relentless juggling act, balancing work, childcare, and the myriad responsibilities that come with single parenthood.

Laura's narrative began to shape policy when she attended a town hall meeting, where she bravely shared her story. She spoke of her struggles with the high cost and limited availability of childcare, the rigidity of her work schedule, and the constant fear of unforeseen emergencies that could disrupt her fragile balance. Laura's story, delivered with raw honesty, resonated with many in the audience, including a local policymaker, Councilwoman Reyes.

Moved by Laura's story and recognizing it as a common thread among her constituents, Councilwoman Reyes began advocating for policies that would support single parents like Laura. She initiated research into the challenges faced by single-parent families in the community, collecting data that highlighted the need for more accessible and affordable childcare solutions.

The councilwoman then proposed a series of policies inspired by Laura's narrative. These included subsidies for childcare tailored to low-income single parents, advocating for local businesses to adopt more flexible work hours, and the establishment of emergency childcare services for unforeseen circumstances. These proposals were not just based on Laura's story; they were a response to the collective voice of single parents in the community, many of whom had similar experiences.

Laura's story also inspired the creation of a community forum for single parents, providing a space for them to share their experiences, offer support, and collectively advocate for change. This group became instrumental in working with local businesses to create family-friendly work environments and in advising the council on the implementation of the new policies.

As these policies took effect, the impact on the community was profound. Single parents like Laura found it easier to manage their work and family responsibilities. The availability of emergency childcare services reduced the stress of unforeseen circumstances, while the subsidies made quality childcare more affordable. Local businesses, initially resistant to the idea of flexible work hours, began to see the benefits in terms of employee morale and productivity.

Laura's story, which started as a personal struggle shared at a town hall meeting, evolved into a catalyst for change, influencing policies that significantly improved the lives of single parents in her community. It demonstrated the power of personal narratives in shaping policy, turning individual experiences into collective action and legislative change.

The transformation of Laura's challenges into actionable policy serves as a poignant example of how living legislation works. It's a testament to the fact that behind every policy are real people with real stories, and when these stories are heard and acted upon, they can lead to meaningful and lasting change. Laura's journey from a struggling single mother to an advocate for change exemplifies the essence of living legislation - the intertwining of personal narratives with public policy to create a more empathetic, responsive, and effective governance.

The case of a community grappling with industrial pollution serves as a poignant example of how local activism, fueled by personal impact, can evolve into significant environmental legislation. A single campaign initiated by a dedicated local activist, driven by the firsthand experience of her community's suffering, can escalate into a movement. This movement, gathering momentum, can lead to comprehensive investigations, revealing systemic issues and prompting the formulation of laws that not only address the immediate problem but also set new benchmarks for environmental safety and corporate responsibility.

In a small town nestled in the heart of a manufacturing region, the local community faced a growing health crisis. For decades, a large factory had been the cornerstone of the town's economy, providing jobs and shaping its identity. However, the factory's operations came with a cost: environmental pollution that increasingly impacted the health of the town's residents.

At the forefront of the battle against this pollution was a local high school science teacher. Observing a worrying trend of respiratory issues among her students, she began to suspect a link to the pollution emitted by the factory. Her concerns were validated by a preliminary study, which suggested a connection between the health problems and the factory's emissions.

Driven by a sense of duty to her students and community, the teacher initiated a grassroots campaign to address the issue. She started with community meetings, which quickly turned into a larger movement as more residents shared their health struggles. Leveraging social media, the campaign gained momentum, drawing attention from local media and environmental advocacy groups.

The movement's key breakthrough came when a comprehensive study, conducted in partnership with a notable environmental organization, revealed dangerously high levels of pollutants in the air and water, linked directly to the factory. This revelation spurred public outrage and a series of town hall meetings where community members demanded action from their local leaders.

The collective effort led to an official investigation into the factory's environmental practices. The story reached state legislators, who were moved by the community's plight. This led to the drafting of new, more stringent environmental legislation. The proposed laws aimed to improve pollution control measures, hold corporations accountable for environmental violations, and involve communities in environmental monitoring.

The small town's campaign became a landmark in environmental advocacy. It led to significant policy changes at the local level and inspired similar movements in other communities facing industrial pollution. The new legislation set new standards for environmental responsibility, emphasizing the importance of corporate accountability and environmental stewardship.

This story of a small town's fight against industrial pollution underscores the power of community activism in shaping public policy. It highlights how the combined voices of concerned individuals can lead to meaningful legal changes, transforming personal experiences into powerful drivers of public health and environmental policy.

Turning personal experiences into public policy is a complex process, akin to alchemical transformation. It requires individuals to step into the arena with their stories, advocating for change amidst a backdrop of competing interests and entrenched power structures. These storytellers must navigate the labyrinthine legislative process, contending with challenges and resistance, yet their resolve to see their narratives shape policy remains unshaken.

The potency of a well-told, heartfelt story in this context cannot be overstated. Such narratives have the power to dismantle barriers, build alliances, and bring a humanizing element to policy debates. They offer compelling, grounded perspectives that can sway public opinion, inspire movements, and motivate lawmakers to action. By rooting policy debates in the lived experiences of those directly impacted, these stories lend urgency and legitimacy to the decision-making process.

Integrating personal narratives into policy-making serves to democratize the process. It challenges the traditional top-down governance model, advocating for a more collaborative approach where policies are shaped in conjunction with those they aim to serve. This approach not only makes legislation more pertinent and effective but also strengthens the bond of trust between the government and its constituents. It signals a commitment to a governance model that values inclusivity, responsiveness, and a deep understanding of the lived experiences of the citizenry.

Living legislation is a vivid representation of the transformation of personal experiences into public policy. This dynamic process ensures that laws and regulations are not mere theoretical constructs but living entities that resonate with the everyday realities of those they serve. It's a journey where individual narratives are woven into the fabric of impactful legislation, demonstrating the power of human experience in creating more empathetic and effective governance.

The journey from personal experience to public policy is also a narrative of resilience and empowerment. It highlights the ability of individuals and communities to effect change and influence the course of governance. Each story of struggle and triumph reinforces the idea that everyone has the power to contribute to the shaping of policies that impact their lives and the lives of others.

CHAPTER 9

Carving a Path: Personal Growth in a Public Sector

9.1. Defining Success on Your Own Terms in a Government Career

In the realm of public service, the concept of success extends far beyond the conventional benchmarks of promotions and accolades. Embarking on a government career invites an introspective journey, one where personal values intertwine with professional aspirations. This chapter delves into the process by which individuals in the public sector can forge their unique paths. By aligning their career trajectories with their deepest convictions and aspirations, they can create a fulfilling and impactful journey in government service.

This unique landscape of the public sector, characterized by a vast array of roles and responsibilities, offers unparalleled opportunities for personal and professional growth. Unlike the private sector, where success is often gauged by profit margins and market dominance, success in government work is predominantly measured by the impact made on policies, communities, and individual lives. Success here is about crafting a legacy in sync with the ethos of public service, fundamentally grounded in serving the greater good.

Analyzing data from various government employee satisfaction surveys uncovers a compelling trend. Individuals who align their personal values with their professional roles often report higher levels of job satisfaction and personal fulfillment. This alignment transcends the mere comfort of a job, resonating deeply with the core purpose of one's work. For example, a study by the Public Administration Review demonstrates that public servants who view their job as a platform for positive societal contributions tend to experience long-term career satisfaction.[70]

Success in government service, for many, is defined by making tangible differences. This might manifest in the smiles of community members benefiting from their work, the seamless functioning of civic systems, or the enactment of laws that protect and empower marginalized groups. Every role, ranging from administrative assistants to high-ranking officials, has the potential to contribute significantly to this tapestry of change.[71]

However, this path is laden with its own set of challenges. The journey involves navigating the complexities of bureaucracy, maintaining integrity amidst political pressures, and balancing personal beliefs with professional responsibilities. These challenges offer fertile ground for personal growth. Overcoming these hurdles not only strengthens one's character but also deepens their commitment to the values of public service.

Personal growth within the public sector often entails a continuous cycle of learning and adapting. The government landscape is in a state of constant flux, influenced by technological innovations, shifts in policy, and societal changes. To maintain relevance and effectiveness, public servants must stay informed and adaptable, seeking further education, engaging in professional development, and keeping abreast of current affairs.

Defining success on one's own terms also involves recognizing the importance of work-life balance. The demanding nature of public service work can often blur the boundaries between professional and personal lives. Striking a balance, prioritizing self-care, and nurturing personal relationships are crucial for long-term success and overall well-being.

This chapter will explore the stories of various individuals who have defined success in their unique ways within the public sector. These narratives provide not only inspiration but also practical insights into navigating a government career with integrity, purpose, and fulfillment. Emerging from these stories are themes of resilience, creativity, and a profound commitment to public service, essential for anyone aiming to carve a rewarding and enriching path in the public sector.

Remember, a career in public service is as much about personal growth as it is about professional achievements. It's about discovering your voice, standing firm in your values, and incrementally making a difference in the world. Each step on this journey contributes to a larger narrative of change and impact, resonating with the core values of public service.

Section Summary[1]:

Navigating a career within the complex tapestry of government work necessitates a distinctive definition of success—one that is personalized and aligned with the intrinsic values that call one to public service. The journey through the public sector is less a linear path and more an expedition marked by the milestones of personal fulfillment, ethical integrity, and societal impact.

Here are key aspects to consider when defining success in a government career:

Identify Core Values: Begin with introspection to understand your core motivations for choosing public service. Whether it's to uphold justice, advance education, or protect the environment, let these values guide your career choices and aspirations.

---

[1] For those inspired to further explore and enrich their journeys within public service or other bureaucratic environments, additional resources and guidance await. Visit theGovCoach.com for a deeper dive into strategies and tools designed to empower your career path. Here, you'll find a wealth of information dedicated to helping you plan, develop, and enhance your role in the realm of public service, providing you with the insights and support needed to navigate and thrive in these dynamic fields.

Set Impact Goals: Rather than focusing solely on promotions or salary increments, set goals related to the impact you wish to have. This could involve influencing a particular policy area, improving services in underserved communities, or mentoring the next generation of public servants.

Seek Fulfillment Over Title: Pursue roles that offer a sense of fulfillment and purpose, even if they don't come with a prestigious title. Engaging in work that resonates with your passions can yield greater satisfaction and a sense of accomplishment.

Embrace Lifelong Learning: View each role and project as an opportunity to learn and grow. Continuous learning can come from formal education, on-the-job experiences, or cross-sector collaborations, each enriching your ability to serve effectively.

Measure Progress Personally: Track your career progress based on personal benchmarks rather than external validation. Reflect regularly on the skills you've acquired, the networks you've built, and the difference you've made in your field.

Cultivate Resilience: Recognize that setbacks and challenges are part of the journey. Resilience is forged in the face of adversity, and learning from difficult experiences can be a significant measure of success.

Balance Ambition with Service: While ambition is a driving force, temper it with a commitment to service. Strive for excellence in your role with the understanding that success is also about the welfare and betterment of the community and nation.

Foster Collaborative Success: Success in government often stems from collaboration. Seek to build and be part of teams where collective achievements are celebrated and each member's contribution is valued.

Lead with Integrity: In public service, integrity is paramount. Define success not just by the outcomes you achieve, but by the manner in which you achieve them—transparently, honestly, and ethically.

Reflect and Adapt: Regularly take stock of your career trajectory and be willing to adapt your definition of success as you grow personally and professionally. What matters is that your career aligns with your evolving understanding of purpose and public service.

By redefining success in a government career on your own terms, you'll likely find that your impact extends beyond the confines of your immediate role, contributing to a legacy of service that persists long after you've moved on. This approach transforms the pursuit of personal career achievements into a lifelong mission of public service, marked by dedication, adaptability, and a relentless commitment to the common good.

9.2. Mentorship Moments: Learning from the Personal Successes of Others

In the multifaceted realm of public service, the role of mentorship emerges as a guiding light, leading individuals through the complexities and uncertainties of government bureaucracy. This section delves deep into the transformative impact of mentorship within the public sector, examining how insights and lessons learned from the experiences of accomplished individuals can profoundly influence one's career trajectory and personal development.

Mentorship in the government sector transcends the boundaries of mere professional advice. It acts as a critical channel for the transfer of values, skills, and profound insights, all of which are vital for effectively navigating the unique challenges posed by public service. This process involves the transfer of wisdom from seasoned mentors to the next generation of leaders, establishing a continuum of knowledge and experience that not only enhances individual careers but also enriches the entire fabric of public service.

Mentorship within government manifests in various forms, ranging from structured mentorship programs to more casual, anecdotal exchanges. These mentor-mentee interactions are invaluable, offering a window into the internal mechanics of government and furnishing practical strategies for overcoming bureaucratic hurdles, ethical complexities, and the intricacies of policy-making.

The narratives of successful mentors in government serve as more than career guides; they are stories of resilience, flexibility, and a deep-seated dedication to public service. These accounts act as tangible illustrations of maintaining integrity, nurturing innovation, and developing emotional intelligence in a setting often marked by stringent regulations and procedural constraints.

An exemplary case is the story of a senior policy advisor who took a junior analyst under their wing. This mentorship was comprehensive, encompassing not only the technical aspects of policy formulation but also the nuanced art of political maneuvering, the balance between personal beliefs and professional responsibilities, and the critical role of empathy in the process of policy-making. This mentorship profoundly transformed the young analyst's approach to their role, fostering a strong sense of purpose and a refined understanding of the impact and significance of their work.

The story of this senior policy advisor and junior analyst represents a quintessential example of the transformative power of mentorship in the public sector. The advisor, a seasoned professional with decades of experience in policy formulation and implementation, recognized the potential in a young, enthusiastic analyst who had recently joined the team. This junior analyst, eager to make a mark in the world of public service, was ripe for guidance but lacked the intricate knowledge of the bureaucratic and political landscape that only experience can provide.

The senior advisor, known for their strategic acumen and empathetic approach to policy-making, saw in the young analyst not just an employee but a future leader. The advisor initiated the mentorship informally, inviting the analyst to participate in high-level meetings and policy discussions. These sessions were eye-openers for the junior analyst, exposing them to the complexities of government work that went far beyond the theoretical knowledge they had acquired in their academic training.

As the mentorship progressed, the senior advisor delved into the subtleties of policy formulation. They emphasized the importance of understanding the political context in which policies are made and implemented, illustrating how the best-intended policies can falter without savvy political maneuvering. The advisor shared stories of past policy successes and failures, dissecting each case to highlight the interplay of policy content, stakeholder engagement, and political will.

One of the key lessons imparted by the advisor was the balance between personal beliefs and professional responsibilities. In the public sector, this balance is often delicate and challenging to maintain. The advisor, through their own experiences, demonstrated how to navigate this balance, making decisions that align with personal ethics while fulfilling professional duties. They encouraged the analyst to develop a personal ethical framework to guide their decision-making in complex situations.

Another critical area of focus was the role of empathy in policymaking. The senior advisor highlighted that policies are not just about laws and regulations; they are about people and their lives. They mentored the analyst on how to listen to and understand the needs and perspectives of various stakeholders, from government officials to the citizens affected by the policies. This approach transformed the young analyst's perspective, making them see their role not just as a job but as a means to impact lives positively.

The mentorship also included practical skills training, such as writing policy briefs, conducting stakeholder analyses, and developing communication strategies. The senior advisor provided feedback on the analyst's work, offering constructive criticism and encouragement. This hands-on approach rapidly enhanced the analyst's skills, making them a valuable asset to the team.

Over time, the mentorship evolved into a profound professional relationship. The junior analyst grew in confidence and capability, taking on more significant projects and responsibilities. They began to embody the values and skills imparted by their mentor, becoming an advocate for empathetic and strategic policymaking within their department.

The story of this mentorship is not just about the professional growth of a junior analyst but also about the perpetuation of a legacy. The senior advisor, through their mentorship, passed on a wealth of knowledge and experience, ensuring that the principles of strategic, ethical, and empathetic policy-making continue to influence government work for years to come. This narrative exemplifies how mentorship in the public sector can shape careers, influence policy, and, ultimately, impact society.

An inspiring example of mentorship in the public sector can be found in the story of a young environmental researcher and a seasoned environmental policy expert. The young researcher, recently graduated with a Ph.D. in environmental science, joined a federal environmental agency and was eager to apply her academic knowledge to real-world policy. The policy expert, with decades of experience in shaping environmental regulations, noticed the potential and the challenges faced by the young scientist in understanding the policy landscape.

Their mentorship began with the policy expert involving the young scientist in a significant project aimed at developing new policies to combat urban air pollution. This project served as a practical learning ground, where the young scientist was exposed to the complexities of policy analysis and the balancing act between scientific data and various socio-economic and political considerations.

A key learning experience was during stakeholder meetings, where the policy expert demonstrated how to manage diverse interests and find common ground among different groups, including government bodies, industry stakeholders, and environmental groups. The young scientist observed the intricate process of negotiations and consensus-building, crucial skills in policy development.

The mentorship expanded beyond this project, as the policy expert guided the young scientist in navigating the organizational landscape, building a professional network, and identifying pathways for career growth. He emphasized the importance of continuous learning and adapting to new environmental challenges and policy shifts.

Under this mentorship, the young researcher transitioned from a scientific focus to becoming a well-rounded environmental policy expert. Their collaborative efforts on the air pollution project resulted in impactful policy changes, reducing urban pollution levels significantly.

The relationship between the young scientist and the policy expert evolved into a lifelong professional bond, with the expert providing ongoing advice and support, extending even to personal growth and work-life balance.

As the young scientist's career progressed, she took on the role of a mentor herself, passing on the knowledge and values she gained to new professionals in the field, continuing the cycle of mentorship and growth in the public sector.

This story illustrates the transformative impact of mentorship in bridging the gap between academic research and practical policy implementation, demonstrating the power of experienced guidance in shaping effective public servants and impactful policies.

Mentorship is also instrumental in promoting diversity and inclusion within the public sector. By offering support and guidance to individuals from diverse backgrounds, mentorship initiatives work to dismantle barriers, fostering equitable opportunities for advancement. This approach ensures that a broad range of perspectives is acknowledged and incorporated into public service, thereby enhancing policy decisions and outcomes.

In exploring mentorship's contribution to personal growth, we find it encourages introspection, assists in identifying strengths and areas for improvement, and cultivates a culture of continual learning and self-improvement. Mentors often act as reflective surfaces, revealing both the potential and the hurdles faced by their mentees, guiding them towards achieving their highest potential.

Moreover, mentorship in the public sector often transcends professional confines, encompassing broader life lessons and personal growth. Mentors frequently become crucial figures in an individual's life, offering wisdom and support that influence not only career choices but also personal values, ethical positions, and significant life decisions.

Mentorship moments in the public sector are crucial in shaping not only successful careers but also well-rounded, insightful individuals. These relationships enrich the experience of public service, transforming it into a journey marked by continuous learning, self-discovery, and impactful contributions.[74] As we delve into these stories of mentorship, we reveal the true essence of personal growth in public service—a path illuminated by the collective wisdom of experienced public servants, paving the way for the next generation of dedicated government professionals.

Section Coaching: Mentorship Moments: Learning from the Personal Successes of Others - Checklist

Identify Potential Mentors: Look for individuals in your organization or broader public sector network who exhibit qualities you admire and possess experience in areas you wish to develop.

Initiate Contact: Don't hesitate to reach out for guidance. Experienced professionals often appreciate the opportunity to share their knowledge and help shape future leaders.

Set Clear Goals: Determine what you want to gain from the mentorship. Are you looking for career advice, skill development, or insights into navigating the bureaucracy?

Engage in Active Listening: When interacting with your mentor, practice active listening to fully absorb their advice, experiences, and perspectives.

Ask Insightful Questions: Prepare thoughtful questions that encourage your mentor to share relevant experiences and wisdom.

Seek Diverse Perspectives: Consider having multiple mentors to gain a broader range of insights and advice, especially from those with different backgrounds or career paths.

Apply Learned Strategies: Implement the strategies, advice, and solutions provided by your mentors in your work. Reflect on the outcomes and discuss them in subsequent meetings.

Embrace Constructive Feedback: Be open to receiving and acting upon feedback, even when it challenges your current way of thinking or working.

Regularly Review Progress: Periodically review the progress of the mentorship relationship with your mentor to ensure it continues to meet your goals and expectations.

Share Your Experiences: As you grow in your career, share your experiences and lessons learned with colleagues and those you mentor.

Maintain Professionalism and Respect: Always maintain a professional relationship with your mentor, respecting their time and contributions.

Cultivate a Long-Term Relationship: Aim to build a lasting professional relationship with your mentor, as the insights and support can be invaluable throughout your career.

Reflect on Personal and Professional Growth: Regularly reflect on how the mentorship is influencing your personal and professional development.

Give Back: As you advance in your career, consider becoming a mentor to others, passing on the knowledge and support you have received.

Document Key Learnings: Keep a journal or record of key insights, advice, and lessons learned during your mentorship journey for future reference.

Implementing these steps can significantly enhance the mentorship experience, providing a robust foundation for personal and professional growth in the public sector.

9.3. The Balancing Act: Managing Personal Ambitions and Public Expectations

In the diverse and complex world of public service, professionals often find themselves at the crossroads of personal ambition and public expectation. This balancing act, a central theme of Chapter 9.3 of our exploration into personal growth within the public sector, is critical to both the fulfillment of individual aspirations and the delivery of effective public service.

The public sector, by its very nature, demands a unique blend of personal commitment and a dedication to the greater good. For many, this environment presents a challenging yet rewarding opportunity to merge personal goals with public needs. However, navigating this landscape requires a nuanced understanding of both the limitations and possibilities inherent within government roles.

One of the primary challenges faced by public servants is aligning personal career goals with the objectives and constraints of government work. Unlike private enterprises, where personal ambition might closely align with company growth, public service demands a more intricate balancing act. Here, success is often measured not just by personal advancement but by the impact one has on the community and the effectiveness of service delivery.

For instance, consider the story of a young urban planner passionate about sustainable development. In a government role, this planner might encounter systemic challenges and bureaucratic hurdles that could dampen personal enthusiasm. However, by understanding the broader impact of their work on city development and environmental sustainability, they can align their personal ambitions with public expectations, finding fulfillment in incremental progress and long-term impact.

The story of Alex, a young and idealistic urban planner, vividly illustrates the complex interplay between personal ambition and public expectation in government service. Alex's passion for sustainable development was more than just a career choice; it was a deep-rooted commitment to shaping a greener, more livable city. However, upon joining the municipal government's planning department, Alex quickly encountered the realities of public sector work.

In the beginning, Alex's days were filled with excitement at the prospect of implementing innovative sustainability projects. But as time passed, the realities of bureaucratic processes, budget constraints, and political dynamics began to surface. Alex's ambitious plans for extensive green spaces, eco-friendly public transportation, and renewable energy initiatives ran into a web of red tape and resistance from various stakeholders.

One of the first major projects Alex undertook was the development of a city park designed to provide green space while also serving as a hub for community activities. Alex envisioned a space that combined aesthetic appeal with environmental functionality, featuring native plants, rain gardens, and solar-powered lighting. However, the proposal was met with skepticism from some city council members concerned about costs and maintenance. Local business owners were apprehensive about the potential disruption during construction.

Feeling disheartened but not defeated, Alex began to realize that success in this role would not come from grand, sweeping changes but through careful negotiation, patience, and incremental progress. Alex spent months meeting with community groups, council members, and local businesses, listening to their concerns and adjusting the park's design to accommodate various interests. Alex also worked tirelessly to secure grants and foster partnerships with local environmental organizations to offset costs and ensure long-term sustainability of the park.

Through this process, Alex learned the art of compromise and the importance of building alliances. The urban planner understood that each small victory was a step towards the larger goal of sustainable urban development. The park, though smaller than initially envisioned, became a beloved community space and a testament to what could be achieved within the confines of government work.

This experience was transformative for Alex. It was a lesson in the complexities of policy-making and the importance of resilience. Alex began to approach projects with a more strategic mindset, seeking out allies early on and being prepared to adapt plans as needed. The planner also became a mentor to newer members of the department, sharing insights on how to navigate the unique challenges of public service while staying true to one's personal convictions.

Alex's story, emblematic of many in public service, highlights the delicate balance between personal aspirations and the realities of government work. It demonstrates that while the path to change in the public sector may be slower and more winding than in other fields, it can be equally, if not more, rewarding. It's a testament to the impact one can have when personal ambitions are aligned with public expectations, contributing positively to the community and the environment.

Another aspect of this balancing act involves managing the expectations of various stakeholders. Public servants often have to navigate the interests of political leaders, community groups, and other agencies. The ability to mediate these interests, while maintaining personal integrity and adhering to one's ethical compass, is a skill that is honed over time and through experience.

Developing this skill often involves learning to communicate effectively, advocate for necessary changes, and build coalitions to support initiatives. It also means being flexible and adaptable, ready to shift strategies as policies and priorities change within the government landscape.

Consider the story of Maya, a public health official tasked with overseeing a city-wide initiative to improve public health outcomes. Maya's journey exemplifies the intricate task of balancing personal convictions with the multifaceted expectations of various stakeholders in the public sector.

Maya's project was ambitious: to reduce the rates of diabetes and heart disease in the city by promoting healthier lifestyles. The plan involved creating more public green spaces for exercise, running public awareness campaigns about healthy eating, and partnering with local schools to improve nutrition in cafeterias. However, Maya quickly encountered obstacles in the form of conflicting interests and bureaucratic hurdles.

Political leaders, while supportive of the initiative in principle, were cautious about endorsing any measures that might be perceived as infringing upon personal freedoms or upsetting influential business groups, such as fast-food chains. Community groups had varied interests; some were enthusiastic about the health initiative, while others were skeptical, viewing it as government overreach into personal choices. Additionally, there were challenges within Maya's own agency, where resources were limited, and some colleagues were resistant to change.

Maya realized that to move this initiative forward, it would require more than just expertise in public health; it would necessitate skilled negotiation, diplomacy, and the ability to build and maintain a coalition of diverse stakeholders. Maya began by organizing a series of community meetings to understand the concerns and expectations of different groups. These meetings were eye-opening, revealing a spectrum of views and ideas that Maya hadn't fully considered.

To address political concerns, Maya worked to frame the initiative in a way that aligned with the broader city goals of economic development and community well-being, demonstrating how healthier citizens could lead to a more vibrant, productive city. Maya also engaged local businesses, proposing collaborations that would allow them to be part of the solution, such as sponsoring community health events or introducing healthier options in their establishments.

Within the agency, Maya advocated for the initiative by illustrating its long-term benefits and aligning it with the agency's mission. By demonstrating how the initiative could be a model for other cities and attract positive attention, Maya was able to garner more support and resources from hesitant colleagues.

Throughout this process, Maya remained adaptable, willing to modify aspects of the initiative to address valid concerns while maintaining the core objectives. This flexibility, combined with a commitment to open communication and collaboration, allowed Maya to gradually build a broad coalition in support of the initiative.

The culmination of these efforts was a series of successful community health fairs, widespread adoption of healthier menus in school cafeterias, and the opening of several new community gardens and exercise facilities across the city. While the path was fraught with challenges, Maya's ability to navigate the complex web of interests and expectations led to meaningful and lasting improvements in public health.

Maya's story highlights the crucial skill of balancing personal ambitions with the myriad expectations in the public sector. By effectively communicating, building coalitions, and staying adaptable, public servants like Maya can navigate the intricate dynamics of government work to create impactful and positive change.

Moreover, public servants must often reconcile the slow pace of change in government with their own aspirations for rapid progress and innovation. This can be particularly challenging for those who enter public service with a desire to make immediate, large-scale changes. Understanding the nature of policy-making, the importance of due process, and the value of patience and persistence is key to maintaining motivation and effectiveness in these roles.

In fostering personal growth within this context, it is crucial to set realistic goals, remain open to learning and adaptation, and seek mentorship and guidance from experienced professionals who have successfully navigated these waters. Engaging in continuous professional development, staying informed about changes in policy and administration, and actively seeking opportunities for innovation within the scope of one's role are all strategies that can help in balancing personal ambitions with public expectations.

Managing personal ambitions within the public sector requires a delicate balancing act, where individual goals must be aligned with the broader mission of public service. To successfully navigate this landscape, public servants must cultivate a deep understanding of their own aspirations and how these intersect with public expectations.

Setting Realistic Goals: Begin by setting clear, achievable goals for your career. Understand that progress in the public sector can be incremental and often requires patience. Set milestones that are realistic, considering the constraints and possibilities of your role. For example, a young environmental engineer might aim to implement a pilot project for sustainable energy within their first two years, rather than expecting large-scale changes immediately.

Understanding the Bigger Picture: Recognize that every role in public service contributes to a larger mission. Whether you are drafting policies, managing city infrastructure, or providing social services, your work impacts the lives of citizens. This perspective can help maintain enthusiasm and commitment, even when facing bureaucratic challenges.

Continuous Learning and Adaptation: The public sector is dynamic, with changing policies, technologies, and societal needs. Stay informed and adaptable. Continuous learning through workshops, courses, and conferences can keep your skills relevant and enhance your ability to innovate within your role.

Seeking Mentorship: Engage with mentors who have navigated similar paths. They can provide valuable insights into managing expectations, overcoming challenges, and achieving fulfillment in public service. Their experiences can serve as a guide and inspiration.

Building Networks: Cultivate relationships within and outside your organization. Networks can provide support, open up new opportunities, and offer diverse perspectives that can enrich your understanding of public service.

Advocating for Change: While understanding the limitations of your role, don't be afraid to advocate for necessary changes. Be a voice for innovation and improvement within your department or agency. This could involve proposing new initiatives, suggesting process improvements, or participating in policy discussions.

Balancing Professional and Personal Life: Public service can be demanding. It's important to maintain a healthy work-life balance, ensuring that your personal well-being and relationships are nurtured alongside your professional responsibilities.

Reflecting on Impact: Regularly take time to reflect on the impact of your work. Celebrate the successes, no matter how small, and learn from the setbacks. This reflection can provide motivation and a sense of achievement, reinforcing the value of your contributions to public service.

Managing personal ambitions in the public sector involves a thoughtful approach that balances individual aspirations with the realities and responsibilities of public service. It's about finding fulfillment in contributing to the greater good while pursuing personal growth and development. This chapter offers insights and strategies to help public servants navigate this journey, fostering a career that is both personally rewarding and beneficial to the community

CHAPTER 10

Reimagining the Future: Personal Visions for Public Reform

10.1. Dreaming Big Within the System: Visionaries of the Public Sector

In the realm of government, where adherence to procedures and protocols is paramount, the emergence of visionary innovators has often been the catalyst for transformative reforms. These trailblazers, adept at melding creative ideas with a profound comprehension of bureaucratic intricacies, have left indelible marks on society.

The story of the municipal housing department manager, Jordan, begins in a city marred by increasing rates of homelessness. The traditional approaches—short-term shelters and temporary assistance—were proving inadequate. Jordan, driven by a combination of compassion and a deep-seated belief in systemic change, envisioned something revolutionary: a comprehensive program that not only provided housing but also addressed the root causes of homelessness.

Jordan's proposal, dubbed "Homes and Hopes," was a multifaceted program. At its core, it offered affordable housing, but it was the additional layers that made it groundbreaking. The program integrated vocational training to equip the homeless with job skills, coupled with mental health services to address underlying psychological issues. This holistic approach was novel in its attempt to provide not just a roof over the heads but a path to self-sufficiency and dignity.

Initially, "Homes and Hopes" was met with skepticism. The city council was wary of the budgetary implications, and some community members doubted its practicality. Jordan faced a challenging task in convincing stakeholders that this innovative approach was not only feasible but also necessary.

What set Jordan apart was their extensive knowledge of the bureaucratic landscape. Having served in various government positions, they understood the nuances of policy-making, budget allocation, and stakeholder engagement. Jordan began by methodically building a case for "Homes and Hopes," gathering data on homelessness trends, studying similar successful models in other cities, and outlining a detailed plan that demonstrated the program's long-term financial and societal benefits.

Jordan then embarked on a campaign to win support. They met with city council members individually, presenting the compelling data and addressing their concerns. They engaged with community leaders and organizations, listening to their input and adapting the program to better suit the community's needs. Jordan also sought innovative funding solutions, tapping into federal grants, local charities, and even proposing a public-private partnership model to reduce the financial burden on the city.

The turning point came when a pilot version of "Homes and Hopes" was launched in a small district. The success of this pilot, evident in its positive impact on participants' lives, was the proof Jordan needed. Gradually, skepticism turned to endorsement, and the program received the green light for city-wide implementation.

"Homes and Hopes" became more than just a program; it evolved into a symbol of progressive change. It showcased how a blend of empathy, innovative thinking, and bureaucratic savvy could lead to impactful solutions. The program's success caught the attention of other cities facing similar challenges, and Jordan was invited to share their insights and experiences.

This story not only highlights Jordan's innovative approach but also serves as a powerful reminder of the potential within public service. It shows how a deep understanding of the system, combined with a willingness to push boundaries, can lead to significant, positive change. Jordan's journey from a concept to a city-wide initiative exemplifies the transformative power of visionary thinking within the confines of government bureaucracy.

In a mid-sized town grappling with the rising tide of the opioid crisis, a seasoned public health official, Dr. Taylor, stood at the forefront of a transformative campaign. The challenge was immense: opioids had seeped into the fabric of the community, leaving a trail of addiction, health complications, and even fatalities. Dr. Taylor, however, was not deterred. With years of experience in public health and a passion for community welfare, they embarked on an ambitious mission to turn the tide against this crisis.

Dr. Taylor's strategy was comprehensive and multifaceted, designed to address the opioid issue from multiple angles. The core of the plan was the establishment of specialized treatment centers, which were to serve not just as places for medical detoxification but as hubs for holistic healing. These centers combined traditional medical treatments with psychological support, offering counseling, therapy, and long-term addiction management plans.

Understanding that the battle against opioids extended beyond the confines of treatment centers, Dr. Taylor also focused on community engagement and education. They spearheaded the training of community health workers, equipping them with the knowledge and tools to identify early signs of opioid abuse, provide initial counseling, and refer individuals to specialized care. This grassroot-level intervention was crucial in early detection and prevention.

To amplify the impact, Dr. Taylor initiated widespread public awareness campaigns. Utilizing various media outlets, these campaigns aimed to destigmatize addiction, educate the public about the dangers of opioid misuse, and inform them about available treatment options.

The messaging was crafted to resonate with different segments of the community, from teenagers and parents to educators and employers.

The linchpin of Dr. Taylor's strategy was their data-driven approach. Recognizing the power of evidence in swaying policy decisions, they meticulously gathered data on opioid abuse patterns in the community, success rates of different treatment modalities, and the socioeconomic impact of the crisis. Armed with this data, Dr. Taylor approached policymakers, effectively communicating the urgency of the situation and the need for substantial support and funding.

The results of this initiative were profound. Within a year, the town saw a noticeable decline in opioid-related emergencies and hospital admissions. The treatment centers reported higher rates of successful addiction management, and community health workers became vital links in the healthcare chain, offering support and guidance to numerous individuals and families.

But perhaps the most significant impact was the shift in public perception. The conversation around opioid addiction changed from a narrative of blame and shame to one of understanding and support. People began to view addiction as a health issue rather than a moral failing, which encouraged more individuals to seek help without fear of stigma.

Dr. Taylor's story is a testament to the power of a well-rounded, informed approach to public health crises. It demonstrates that with the right combination of expertise, dedication, and a deep understanding of the community, public health officials can spearhead meaningful and lasting change. This narrative not only serves as an inspiration for other public health professionals facing similar challenges but also shines a light on the potential of thoughtful, comprehensive public health strategies in making tangible differences in people's lives.

In a coastal city known for its vibrant culture and diverse population, a significant challenge loomed: the escalating issue of environmental degradation and its impact on public health. At the heart of the city's response was a dynamic environmental health officer, Bryan, who possessed a unique vision for a greener, healthier urban landscape.

Bryan had long been an advocate for environmental sustainability, combining a deep understanding of ecological science with a passion for public health. Witnessing the city's struggle with pollution, waste management issues, and the resulting health problems, Bryan was determined to orchestrate a change. The plan was ambitious: to transform the city into a model of environmental health, balancing urban development with ecological preservation.

The first step in Bryan's plan involved tackling the city's chronic air and water pollution. This entailed a comprehensive strategy that included stricter regulations on industrial emissions, incentives for businesses to adopt cleaner technologies, and a significant investment in green infrastructure. Bryan worked closely with local industries, negotiating and guiding them towards more sustainable practices, emphasizing the long-term benefits for both the environment and their businesses.

Parallel to these efforts, Bryan initiated a massive public green space project. This project wasn't just about creating parks; it was about integrating nature into the urban fabric. These green spaces were designed to be more than just aesthetic enhancements; they were ecosystems that supported biodiversity, provided residents with recreational areas, and improved the city's air quality.

A critical component of Bryan's vision was community involvement. Understanding the importance of public buy-in, Bryan launched a series of community engagement programs. These programs educated citizens about the importance of environmental health and encouraged their participation in initiatives like urban gardening, recycling drives, and community clean-ups. Schools and local organizations became active participants in these programs, fostering a city-wide culture of environmental stewardship.

Another significant challenge Bryan faced was the city's outdated waste management system. To address this, Bryan spearheaded the development of a new waste management policy, focusing on recycling and composting. Partnering with technology firms, Bryan helped introduce innovative waste processing methods that significantly reduced landfill waste and turned organic waste into compost for the city's green spaces.

Bryan's efforts extended beyond immediate environmental concerns, touching upon long-term public health. They collaborated with public health officials to track the impact of environmental policies on the city's health indicators, such as respiratory and cardiovascular diseases. This data-driven approach provided tangible evidence of the positive impact of a healthier environment, reinforcing the need for continued investment in sustainable urban practices.

Over the years, Bryan's vision materialized into reality. The city's air and water quality improved markedly, green spaces flourished, and a new culture of environmental consciousness took root among the citizens. The city not only became a healthier place to live but also stood as a beacon of sustainable urban development, inspiring other cities worldwide.

Bryan's story is a powerful example of how visionary thinking, grounded in a profound understanding of environmental science and public health, can lead to transformative changes in a community. It illustrates the potential of dedicated public servants to not only address pressing challenges but also to reimagine and reshape the future of urban living. This narrative serves as a source of inspiration and a blueprint for others in the public sector looking to make a lasting impact in their communities.

These examples illustrate that dreaming big within the public sector involves more than just ideation; it requires the acumen and resolve to make these ideas a reality. It's a confluence of creativity, strategic planning, and an unwavering commitment to public service.

These individuals navigated the complex terrain of government to effect enduring change. Their journeys are a testament to the fact that with a combination of innovative thought, perseverance, and a thorough understanding of the system, it is possible to reshape the future and leave a lasting legacy in public service. These narratives provide valuable lessons and inspiration for anyone in the public sector aiming to make a substantial impact, showing that visionary thinking, coupled with practical action, can lead to meaningful and lasting reforms.

10.2. Sustainability Starts with Us: Personal Responsibility in Global Policy

The pursuit of sustainable global policy, deeply rooted in the actions and responsibilities of individuals within the public sector, is a testament to the power of personal commitment in shaping the world's future. This section of our book delves into how the choices and ethics of public servants are pivotal in implementing effective sustainability policies on a global scale, emphasizing that true change often starts with individual actions.

In today's world, where environmental challenges loom large, traditional bureaucratic methods alone are insufficient. A new mindset is required, one where public servants view themselves not merely as implementers of policy but as proactive contributors to the sustainability mission. This mindset demands a fusion of personal conviction with professional duty, bridging the gap between individual actions and global impacts.

This approach underscores that every decision in the public sector, no matter its scale, contributes to the broader sustainability agenda. Simple acts, like adopting green office practices or championing eco-friendly policies, accumulate to create significant systemic shifts. The aggregate impact of such actions can catalyze substantial environmental progress.

For example, a city planner's commitment to sustainability resulted in a revolutionary 'green blueprint' for urban development. This planner's personal initiative led to the integration of sustainable practices, such as energy-efficient buildings, green transport networks, and eco-friendly waste systems, fundamentally transforming the cityscape. This project not only reshaped the city's physical environment but also served as a model for other cities, showcasing the profound influence of individual initiative on broader policy changes.

The story of the city planner, Sam, who spearheaded a 'green blueprint' for urban development, serves as a compelling illustration of how individual commitment can catalyze substantial policy changes and reshape the urban landscape towards sustainability.

Sam, driven by a deep-seated passion for environmental stewardship, recognized the urgent need to address the city's growing ecological footprint. Aware of the escalating challenges of urbanization – pollution, energy consumption, and waste management – Sam envisioned a transformative approach to city planning. This approach aimed to integrate sustainable practices into the very fabric of urban development, ensuring the city's growth was in harmony with environmental conservation.

The 'green blueprint' Sam proposed was ambitious and holistic. It encompassed a wide range of initiatives: constructing energy-efficient buildings that utilized renewable energy sources, developing an extensive network of green transportation options like bike lanes and electric buses, and implementing advanced, eco-friendly waste management systems. Sam's vision extended to the creation of green spaces within the city, such as parks and community gardens, to enhance the urban ecosystem and provide residents with much-needed greenery.

However, turning this vision into reality was not without challenges. Sam faced initial skepticism from city officials and stakeholders, who were concerned about the feasibility and budgetary implications of such a sweeping overhaul. To address these concerns, Sam embarked on a meticulous campaign of persuasion and education, demonstrating how each aspect of the 'green blueprint' was not only environmentally crucial but also economically viable in the long term.

Sam conducted extensive research to back up the proposal, presenting data on how energy-efficient buildings reduce long-term operational costs, how green transportation networks decrease healthcare expenses by reducing pollution-related illnesses, and how eco-friendly waste systems can be both cost-effective and revenue-generating.

One of the pivotal moments in Sam's journey was securing the buy-in from key stakeholders. Sam organized workshops and meetings with community leaders, business owners, and residents, listening to their concerns and suggestions. By incorporating their feedback into the planning process, Sam built a sense of community ownership over the project, which was crucial in gaining widespread support.

As the 'green blueprint' began to materialize, the city witnessed a remarkable transformation. Energy-efficient buildings started dotting the skyline, green transport options became a common sight, and waste management practices improved drastically. The city's air quality improved, and there was a noticeable increase in public health and well-being.

The success of the project in Sam's city soon caught the attention of other urban centers. It became a benchmark for sustainable urban development, inspiring similar initiatives in cities across the country and even globally. Sam's dedication and strategic approach had not only transformed their own city but had also set a precedent for others to follow.

Sam's story is a testament to the power of individual initiative in driving policy change. It underscores the potential of personal commitment in the public sector to bring about lasting, positive impacts on both local and global scales. Sam's journey from a passionate city planner to a pioneer of sustainable urban development exemplifies how personal responsibility and professional action can align to create a more sustainable and livable future.

The story of Tyre, a procurement officer in a mid-sized city's municipal government, exemplifies the significant impact an individual can have in championing sustainability within the public sector. Tyre's role involved overseeing the procurement of goods and services for various city departments, a position that, while seemingly routine, held immense potential for promoting eco-friendly practices.

Tyre, a long-time advocate for environmental conservation, recognized the opportunity to influence the city's ecological footprint through their procurement choices. Mindful of the environmental impact of products and services, Tyre began to prioritize eco-friendly options. This shift entailed choosing suppliers who offered sustainably sourced materials, opting for energy-efficient equipment, and selecting services that adhered to environmental best practices.

Initially, Tyre's approach faced resistance. Concerns were raised about the cost implications of choosing green products over more traditional, and often cheaper, alternatives. To address these concerns, Tyre embarked on a data-driven campaign to demonstrate the long-term economic and environmental benefits of sustainable procurement. Tyre highlighted how eco-friendly products, though sometimes more expensive upfront, offered greater durability and efficiency, leading to cost savings over time.

Moreover, Tyre's commitment to sustainable procurement began to influence market trends within the city. As the municipal government consistently chose eco-friendly products, suppliers were incentivized to offer more sustainable options to remain competitive. This shift gradually permeated the local market, with businesses and residents increasingly opting for eco-friendly products, contributing to a broader culture of sustainability in the community.

Alongside these efforts, Tyre recognized the importance of educating colleagues and stakeholders about the benefits and necessity of sustainability. Tyre organized workshops and training sessions for city employees, focusing on the principles of sustainable procurement and its positive impact on the environment and public health. These sessions also covered the global implications of local procurement choices, emphasizing how individual actions contribute to broader environmental goals.

Tyre's initiative extended beyond procurement to champion a city-wide sustainability education program. Partnering with local environmental organizations and experts, Tyre helped develop a series of educational materials and events for the public, aimed at raising awareness about sustainability and encouraging environmentally responsible practices among residents and businesses.

The impact of Tyre's efforts was multifaceted. Within the municipal government, there was a noticeable shift towards more sustainable practices in various departments, inspired by the procurement office's example. In the community, there was an increased demand for eco-friendly products and services, catalyzing a shift in local business practices. Perhaps most significantly, Tyre's actions contributed to a heightened collective consciousness about sustainability, fostering a culture where environmental responsibility became a shared value and priority.

Tyre's story illustrates the powerful role individual public servants can play in advocating for and implementing sustainable practices. It demonstrates how a single person's commitment and strategic action can catalyze systemic change, influencing market trends, shaping public opinion, and ultimately contributing to a more sustainable and environmentally conscious community. This narrative serves as a compelling example of how personal responsibility and professional dedication can align to advance sustainability, not just within the confines of a government office but across an entire city and beyond.

The influence of individual public servants in advocating and adhering to sustainable practices is profound. A procurement officer prioritizing eco-friendly products, for instance, sets a precedent that influences market trends and fosters community-wide sustainability.

Additionally, this section highlights the critical role of education and awareness in fostering a culture of sustainability in the public sector. It's imperative for public servants to grasp the principles of sustainability and comprehend the global ramifications of their actions. Continuous education, training programs, and workshops are pivotal in equipping them with the necessary knowledge and skills to make informed, sustainable decisions.

Moreover, public servants in leadership positions carry the responsibility of advocacy and policy influence. Their ability to champion sustainable practices and legislation not only impacts policy but also inspires others in the sector, creating a domino effect towards a sustainable future.

The stories and insights in this section offer a comprehensive perspective on how personal responsibility and individual actions are indispensable for the success of global sustainability policies. They illustrate that while systemic change is vital, the initiation of this change often lies in the hands of individual system members. By embracing personal responsibility and aligning individual actions with larger sustainability goals, public servants become pivotal agents in sculpting a sustainable future for all.

10.3. A Call to Action: Crafting Your Legacy in Government

The journey through public service is not just a career path; it is an opportunity to leave a lasting imprint on society. As we navigate the multifaceted landscape of government work, we find ourselves with the unique potential to create legacies that resonate far beyond our tenure. Crafting a legacy in government hinges on the understanding that our actions, decisions, and policies shape the lives of individuals and the course of communities for years to come.

This pursuit of a lasting legacy in government is rooted in the realization that each decision made, each policy implemented, and each service rendered has the potential to influence lives and societies. It's about understanding the weight of responsibility that comes with public service – the knowledge that what we do today can echo through generations. It's recognizing that whether one is drafting legislation, implementing community programs, or providing essential services, each action contributes to a larger story of societal development.

Public service offers a platform where one's work can significantly influence the direction of societal development. This power to effect change, however, comes with the responsibility to act with foresight, integrity, and a deep sense of duty towards the public good. It calls for a commitment to principles that transcend personal gain, aligning actions with the broader objectives of societal welfare and progress.

In this endeavor, public servants must embrace the role of stewards of the public trust. This means prioritizing the collective interest over personal agendas, ensuring that the policies and programs developed serve the needs of the community, especially the most vulnerable. It's about cultivating an ethos of service that prioritizes the welfare of citizens and the health of the community as a whole.

Creating a legacy in government is not confined to high-ranking positions or headline-making initiatives. It occurs at all levels of public service, through the cumulative impact of everyday decisions and actions. For example, a policy analyst working tirelessly to refine a healthcare reform, a city engineer developing sustainable urban infrastructure, or a social worker advocating for vulnerable populations – each contributes to the tapestry of public service legacy.

These contributions, often unnoticed, are the building blocks of a meaningful legacy. They are the countless hours spent analyzing data to inform policy decisions, the dedication to ensuring that public projects are both efficient and equitable, and the compassion shown in delivering services to those in need. It's in these seemingly small acts that the true essence of public service is found.

A key aspect of this legacy-building is the capacity to envision the future. Visionary public servants look beyond the immediate implications of their work, considering the long-term effects of policies and actions. They strive to address not just the challenges of today but also anticipate and prepare for the needs of tomorrow. This foresight is critical in fields such as environmental policy, urban planning, and public health, where decisions have enduring consequences.

Envisioning the future also involves an awareness of emerging trends and an openness to new ideas. It requires staying informed about advancements in technology, shifts in demographics, and changes in societal values. Visionary public servants are those who can adapt to these changes and envision how they can be harnessed to improve public services and outcomes.

Moreover, crafting a legacy requires a balance between innovation and adherence to core values. The public sector often presents complex challenges that require creative solutions, but these innovations must be grounded in ethical practices and a commitment to public welfare. This balance is crucial in maintaining public trust and ensuring that the legacy left behind is not just impactful but also honorable.

In this pursuit of balance, public servants must navigate the delicate line between pushing boundaries and respecting established principles. It's about finding innovative ways to solve problems while upholding values such as transparency, fairness, and respect for the rule of law. It's recognizing that true innovation in public service is not just about implementing new ideas but doing so in a way that upholds the trust and confidence of the public.

Effective communication and collaboration are also vital in legacy building. The ability to articulate visions, garner support, and work collaboratively across various sectors and communities can significantly amplify the impact of one's work. Collaborative efforts often lead to more comprehensive and inclusive policies, reflecting a diverse range of perspectives and needs.

Collaboration extends beyond working within government agencies; it involves engaging with community members, non-profit organizations, businesses, and other stakeholders. Effective public servants understand that building partnerships and fostering open lines of communication can lead to more innovative and effective solutions. They recognize that the best policies are often those that are developed through a collaborative process that takes into account the views and needs of all affected parties.

Additionally, mentoring and nurturing the next generation of public servants is a profound way to extend one's legacy. By imparting knowledge, sharing experiences, and fostering a culture of excellence and service, seasoned public servants can inspire and equip future leaders to carry forward the mantle of responsible and effective governance.

Mentorship in this context is more than just providing career advice; it's about instilling a sense of duty and a passion for public service. It's about guiding emerging leaders to understand the complexities of government work, the importance of ethical decision-making, and the art of balancing various interests and perspectives. It's about passing on the wisdom gained from years of service, not just to help the next generation succeed professionally, but to ensure they carry on the commitment to serving the public with integrity and dedication.

Reflecting on personal values and motivations is another critical aspect of this journey. Understanding what drives one's dedication to public service can provide clarity and focus, helping to align personal aspirations with public needs. This introspection often leads to more meaningful and fulfilling contributions, as actions are guided by a deep-seated sense of purpose and commitment.

This self-reflection is crucial for public servants to remain grounded and focused on their mission. It's about constantly asking oneself why one chose the path of public service and what impact one hopes to have. This ongoing self-assessment helps to ensure that one's work is not just professionally rewarding but also personally fulfilling and aligned with one's core values.

Crafting a legacy in government is not a pursuit reserved for a select few. It is an opportunity available to every public servant, at every level. It requires a confluence of vision, integrity, collaboration, and a steadfast commitment to the public good. The legacies we leave are the imprints of our dedication to service, our resilience in the face of challenges, and our unwavering commitment to bettering the lives of those we serve. In embracing this responsibility, we not only enrich our professional journeys but also contribute to the greater narrative of societal progress and transformation.

As public servants, we have the privilege and the burden of shaping the world we live in. The decisions we make, the policies we implement, and the services we provide all have the potential to leave a lasting mark on our communities and our world. The question then becomes, what kind of legacy do we wish to leave? How do we want to be remembered, and what impact do we want to have? This chapter invites us to ponder these questions and challenges us to act with the knowledge that our work has the power to create a legacy that endures long after we have left the public stage.

CHAPTER 11

Transformative Leadership

11.1 Leading with Authenticity

In the realm of public service, authenticity is not merely a trait but a fundamental element of transformative leadership. Authenticity extends beyond mere honesty or transparency; it's about a profound alignment between a leader's values, words, and actions. This alignment fosters trust and respect, which are crucial for effective leadership.

In the public sector, the importance of authentic leadership is magnified. It influences the culture of governance and sets a precedent for policy development and implementation. Authentic leaders in government stay true to their core values and principles despite bureaucratic challenges and political pressures. They lead with empathy, understanding, and a genuine commitment to the public good, not just with authority.

A defining quality of authentic leadership is the ability to listen and engage sincerely with others. This involves actively seeking and valuing diverse perspectives and incorporating them into the decision-making process. Authentic leaders recognize that effective governance is a collaborative endeavor and appreciate the insights and contributions of all stakeholders.

Consistency is another key attribute of authentic leadership. In the dynamic world of politics and governance, holding fast to one's values and principles can be challenging. Authentic leaders, however, maintain their convictions, offering stability in times of change and uncertainty. This consistency fosters trust, as constituents and colleagues are clear about their leader's direction and intentions.

Authentic leaders also embrace vulnerability. They are not afraid to acknowledge mistakes or areas for improvement. This openness is not a weakness but a recognition of the complexity of public service and the need for cooperative leadership. By showing vulnerability, leaders can forge stronger connections with their teams and cultivate an environment of mutual support and continuous learning.

Commitment to personal growth and development is intrinsic to authentic leadership. Leaders who are authentic continually strive to improve, motivated by the desire to better serve their communities. They are receptive to feedback, engage in self-reflection, and constantly seek new ways to enhance their leadership efficacy.

One of the most profound impacts of authentic leadership is its ability to inspire and motivate. When leaders are genuine in their actions and intentions, they can kindle a passion for public service in others. They can encourage their teams to exceed expectations and work collectively towards a shared vision of improved communities and a better world.

Authentic leadership is crucial in fostering a culture of integrity and ethical behavior. In an environment where leaders adhere to their values and principles, ethical considerations take precedence in decision-making. This integrity is vital for maintaining public trust and ensuring that government actions are always geared towards the public's best interest.

Authenticity in leadership is about more than personal integrity; it's about cultivating a leadership style rooted in honesty, empathy, and a profound commitment to public service. It involves building relationships based on trust and respect and promoting a culture of collaboration, integrity, and perpetual growth. This chapter explores how authentic leadership can be a potent tool for transforming government and effecting enduring societal change.

11.2 The Ripple Effect of Compassionate Leadership

Compassionate leadership in the public sector is akin to planting seeds of hope and nurturing them into trees of change that provide shelter to many. It's about cultivating an ethos where the emotional well-being of both the served and the server is paramount. When leaders operate from a place of empathy and understanding, their actions create a resonance that permeates through the structure of government, affecting policies and the people behind them. This leadership style is not about relinquishing authority; it is about wielding that authority with a sense of responsibility that extends beyond the mere execution of tasks to the fostering of human dignity.

These leaders exemplify a commitment to service that is personal, palpable, and perennial. They recognize that their decisions have a human cost, and they strive to minimize the hardship that bureaucratic processes can inadvertently impose. By incorporating emotional intelligence into their leadership toolkit, they are able to navigate the often impersonal machinery of government with a personal touch, ensuring that the services rendered are not just efficient but also empathetic.

At the heart of this approach lies the concept of 'servant leadership,' a term coined by Robert K. Greenleaf, which emphasizes the importance of leaders to prioritize the needs of others. Servant leaders seek to ensure that other people's highest priority needs are being served to encourage their development and well-being. This philosophy has proven effective in various public sector organizations, as it fosters an environment of trust and mutual respect, essential ingredients for a productive and harmonious workplace.

The impact of compassionate leadership is far-reaching. It can be seen in the increased engagement of employees who feel that their voices are heard and their contributions valued. This, in turn, translates to a more motivated workforce that is committed to the organization's goals. Such an environment encourages innovation as employees feel secure in expressing new ideas and participating in the decision-making process.

Furthermore, compassionate leadership plays a crucial role in crisis management. When faced with adversity, leaders who respond with understanding and support, rather than blame and punishment, are more likely to steer their teams through challenges successfully. They create a culture of resilience where employees are not afraid to take calculated risks, knowing that their leaders will support them regardless of the outcome.

Statistics and studies across various sectors corroborate the effectiveness of this leadership style. According to the Center for Creative Leadership, organizations led by individuals with high emotional intelligence are 20% more likely to have a satisfied and committed workforce. Moreover, the impact on public trust cannot be overstated. The Edelman Trust Barometer indicates that institutions led by compassionate leaders are more trusted by the public, which is crucial for the legitimacy and effectiveness of government actions.

Leaders who practice compassion understand the power of empathy in public policy. They know that policies crafted with consideration for the people's well-being can have a transformative impact on society. By creating policies that are not only just but also kind, they engender a sense of community and shared purpose among citizens.

In the narratives of these leaders, one finds a common theme: the belief that the strength of a society is measured by how it treats its weakest members. They lead by example, showing that the true measure of leadership is not the accumulation of power but the widespread distribution of hope, opportunity, and compassion.

The ripple effect of compassionate leadership is a legacy that endures. It is reflected in the lives of those touched by the policies and actions of these leaders, in the morale of the teams they lead, and in the societal norms they help to shape. These leaders are the architects of a future where governance is not a cold exercise of power but a warm embrace of collective human potential. They are the champions of a vision where the government is not an imposing structure but a nurturing space that enables every individual to thrive.

11.3 Fostering a Culture of Empathy

The transformative act of instilling a culture of empathy within the structures of government reconfigures the very essence of public institutions, morphing them into entities that breathe with a compassion that is palpable both internally among the workforce and externally among the citizenry they serve. This vital transformation is ignited and fueled by leadership that not only preaches emotional intelligence but practices it, embedding within every policy and interaction a profound sense of shared humanity and understanding.

Leaders committed to an empathetic approach to governance understand intrinsically that those who carry out the day-to-day operations of government are not merely functionaries or placeholders within an organizational chart. These individuals are the lifeblood of the institution, each with their own narrative, their own set of personal triumphs, and challenges. This realization fosters a leadership style that is not content with surface-level engagements but seeks to truly understand — to hear the unspoken, to acknowledge the overlooked, and to act with a compassion that is as informed as it is genuine.

This approach to leadership catalyzes a workplace culture where every team member feels genuinely seen and valued, not just for their productivity but for their humanity. The impact of such a culture on job satisfaction and retention is not speculative but well-documented. Organizations that have excelled in fostering an empathetic work environment have seen quantifiable benefits, outperforming their less emotionally intelligent counterparts significantly. This correlation between empathy and performance is a clarion call to leaders within the public sector to prioritize the emotional well-being of their teams as a strategic imperative.

Empathy within the ranks of government has a far-reaching impact, fostering teams that coalesce not just around shared tasks but shared values and vision. The connection that empathy nurtures among team members transcends the professional milieu, spurring innovation, creativity, and a proactive stance towards challenges. The data is unequivocal: environments where empathy is a core value see higher levels of engagement and innovation, particularly among the younger workforce, who often prioritize meaningful work that resonates with their personal values.

When government agencies embrace empathy, they do more than enhance internal operations; they bridge the gap that so often exists between government and governed. A citizenry that feels heard and respected is more likely to engage positively with their government, to trust its intentions, and to support its initiatives. This trust is the bedrock upon which effective governance is built and is a primary factor in the success or failure of public policies and programs.

Empathetic leadership extends its influence to the very policies that shape the lives of citizens. When leaders consider the lived experiences of the individuals affected by their decisions, they craft policies that are not only effective but also just and compassionate. Such policies reflect a nuanced understanding of the people they are designed to serve, resulting in more equitable and effective governance. The OECD's findings on the integration of empathy into policy development underscore its importance, revealing that policies developed with an empathetic lens are more likely to meet the public's actual needs and are more sustainable over the long term.

The narratives of leaders who have harnessed the power of empathy to drive change within their governments illuminate the path for others to follow. These stories of transformation across all levels of government underscore the profound effects that a single individual's commitment to empathy can achieve. By weaving empathy into the fabric of their institutions, these leaders have not only achieved significant positive change but have also established legacies that will inspire and guide future generations of public servants.

Fostering a culture of empathy necessitates a dedication to continuous personal and institutional development. It calls for leaders to be open to new perspectives, to confront and dismantle prejudices, and to seek out opportunities to connect more deeply with both colleagues and the community at large. Such commitment is essential to transforming government into a powerful agent of good, capable of meeting today's challenges while laying the groundwork for a future built on mutual trust and cooperative endeavor.

As the public sector continues to adapt and evolve, the importance of empathy in its ranks cannot be overstated. It is a cornerstone upon which a truly people-centric government can be built, a strategy that not only enhances the effectiveness and responsiveness of public service but also reaffirms the noblest ideals of what it means to serve the public. In this ever-evolving narrative, empathy emerges not as a luxury but as an indispensable element in the quest to create a government that is not only efficient and effective but also compassionate and just.

Checklist for Fostering a Culture of Empathy in Organizational Leadership

Lead by Example: Embody empathy in your daily actions and interactions. Your team will mirror your behavior.

Active Listening Sessions: Regularly schedule time to listen to your team's concerns, ideas, and feedback. Ensure they feel heard and understood.

Empathy Training: Incorporate empathy training in professional development programs for your staff.

Recognize Individuality: Acknowledge and appreciate the diverse backgrounds and experiences of your team members.

Open Communication Channels: Establish and maintain open lines of communication across all levels of the organization.

Encourage Team Collaboration: Create opportunities for team members to work together, understanding and appreciating each other's roles and contributions.

Empathetic Policy Making: Involve various voices in policy development, ensuring decisions are informed by a broad range of perspectives.

Feedback Mechanisms: Implement effective mechanisms for employees to share their experiences and suggestions safely.

Work-Life Balance: Promote and respect a balance between work and personal life for all employees.

Regular Check-Ins: Conduct regular one-on-one meetings to understand individual challenges and provide support.

Empathetic Conflict Resolution: Handle conflicts by focusing on understanding all sides and finding mutually beneficial solutions.

Supportive Work Environment: Cultivate an environment where employees feel safe to express themselves without fear of judgment or retribution.

Personal Development Focus: Encourage personal growth and self-awareness among your team.

Community Engagement: Involve your organization in community activities to foster a broader sense of empathy and social responsibility.

Promote Inclusivity: Strive for inclusivity in all organizational practices, ensuring every voice is valued and represented.

Transparent Decision-Making: Be open about how and why decisions are made within the organization.

Show Appreciation: Regularly acknowledge and show appreciation for your team's efforts and achievements.

Empathy in Customer Service: Ensure that empathy extends to interactions with the public or clients, enhancing service quality and satisfaction.

Encourage Vulnerability: Create a safe space for employees to share their failures and learn from them without fear of negative consequences.

Ongoing Evaluation: Continuously assess and improve the organization's empathetic practices, staying adaptable to changing needs.

This checklist serves as a guideline for organizational leaders aiming to foster a culture of empathy, enhancing both internal dynamics and public relations, as well as leaders aiming to cultivate a more empathetic styles in enhancing both internal dynamics and external relationships.

CHAPTER 12

The Stewardship of Elected Service

12.1. Answering the Call: The Journey into Elected Office

The entry into elected office often begins with a resonant, personal call to action—a distinct moment or accumulation of experiences that ignites a commitment to serve the public in the most direct way possible. For those who answer this call, the journey is as unique as their fingerprints, yet universal themes of aspiration, adversity, and adaptation weave through their narratives.

Ming-Na's days were often long, starting before the sun rose over the horizon and ending long after it had set. As a social worker, she had dedicated her life to helping others navigate the complexities of life's challenges. It was this profound commitment to service that had planted the seeds of a growing desire to impact her community on a broader scale. However, the decision to transition from advocacy and social work to the rigors of a political campaign was one that required careful contemplation and meticulous planning.

Ming-Na's contemplation about entering the political arena was not just a personal ambition; it was a response to a community's call. Those whose lives she had touched through her years of service saw in her the embodiment of leadership with a human touch. They recognized that her deep understanding of social issues, combined with her natural empathy, could translate into policies that addressed the root causes of community challenges. These individuals, who had witnessed her tireless dedication, became her most ardent advocates, urging her to consider a role where her influence could extend even further.

As Ming-Na entertained the idea, she was fully aware that such a transition was a momentous stride. The responsibilities of public office were manifold, and the expectations were high. She knew that it would take more than just a desire to serve; it would require a comprehensive plan and a firm grasp of the realities of campaigning. Ming-Na approached this with her characteristic thoroughness, seeking advice from those who had walked this path before her. In conversations with mentors and sessions with local elected officials, she delved into the minutiae of campaign life. They spoke candidly about the sacrifices and the unwavering commitment needed, painting a realistic picture of the journey ahead.

Financial considerations stood at the forefront of this venture. Ming-Na was acutely aware that while her passion for service was boundless, her financial resources were not. She had to be practical about the financial implications of a campaign, which meant taking a hard look at her personal finances. Ming-Na sifted through her savings, investments, and expenses, running through scenarios and budgets. She understood that her financial stability was crucial, not just for the campaign, but for her peace of mind and ability to focus on the tasks ahead.

Reaching out within her network, Ming-Na began to sketch out a fundraising strategy. She identified individuals and groups who shared her vision and values, those who understood the transformative potential of her leadership. Ming-Na's approach to fundraising was methodical and personal; she met with potential donors, not just to seek contributions, but to engage them in a dialogue about the future she envisioned for the community. She crafted a narrative that connected her personal journey with her political aspirations, resonating with those who were willing to invest in a campaign that promised meaningful change.

These early stages of campaign planning were as much a test of Ming-Na's resolve as they were a testament to her preparedness. Every step was taken with deliberation and every decision was weighed against her overarching goal of serving the public good. With each mentor's advice and each supporter's pledge, Ming-Na's vision for her campaign became clearer and her resolve stronger. She was not merely planning to run; she was laying the foundation for a movement that would bring the values of empathy and experience to the forefront of governance.

Ming-Na was deeply entrenched in her role as a social worker, a position that came with the profound responsibility of being a lifeline for her clients. Acknowledging her professional obligations, she began to meticulously plan for a transition that would safeguard her clients' interests. She conducted extensive discussions with her colleagues, ensuring they were prepared to provide the same level of care and support. Ming-Na also engaged in knowledge transfer sessions, sharing case histories, and individual care strategies to ensure no detail was overlooked.

Her commitment to her clients was unwavering, and she was determined to leave her current role without causing any disruption to the services they depended on. Ming-Na's ethical compass directed her to make this transition as smooth as possible, a testament to her dedication and the respect she held for her profession and those it served.

As she navigated these intricate professional dynamics, Ming-Na turned her attention to the multifaceted task of campaign planning. Aware that she could not embark on this journey alone, she began assembling a campaign team. She sought individuals who were not only skilled in various facets of campaign management but who also shared her ethos of service and community engagement. This team would be the backbone of her campaign, helping to amplify her message and vision.

The crafting of her campaign message was a thoughtful process. Ming-Na delved into the issues that she had encountered in her social work, issues that were echoed in the lives of the constituents she aspired to represent. Her message was shaped by real stories and real experiences, not abstract concepts. She understood that the problems facing her community required solutions grounded in reality, and her policy positions reflected this understanding.

The strategy for reaching voters was another aspect of the campaign that Ming-Na approached with a blend of innovation and inclusivity. She organized small gatherings in community centers, visited local businesses, and held virtual town halls to connect with a broad spectrum of the electorate. Ming-Na knew that every conversation was an opportunity to listen, learn, and weave the diverse threads of her community into a cohesive vision for change.

Ming-Na's evenings and weekends became a whirlwind of activity, dedicated to building the momentum her campaign needed. Despite the long hours and the ever-growing list of tasks, she found energy in the enthusiasm of her growing number of supporters. Volunteers were drawn to her authenticity and her palpable passion for making a difference. Together, they began to lay the groundwork for a campaign that was not just about winning an election but about igniting a collective movement towards a more responsive and compassionate government.

The very message of her campaign was sculpted from the narratives she had been part of as a social worker. She framed her platform around the actual needs and concerns of her constituents, which she understood intimately. Ming-Na's evenings were filled with drafting speeches, policy outlines, and plans for community engagement. She poured over local issues, aligning her campaign with the voices she heard daily.

Ming-Na's introspective journey led her to a crossroads where self-awareness became as crucial as her policy knowledge. Her preparations extended into the intellectual realm as well. Ming-Na was already well-versed in the social issues that her campaign would focus on, but she delved deeper into the intricacies of policy development and implementation. She enrolled in courses that offered insights into the legislative process, budgeting, and the intersection of local, state, and federal regulations. These educational endeavors were not mere academic pursuits; they were strategic efforts to ensure that her policies were not only well-intentioned but also actionable and grounded in the art of the possible.

When the day came to declare her candidacy officially, Ming-Na stood before her community not just as a candidate but as a testament to the power of thoughtful engagement in public service. Her campaign was a narrative of evolution, of a personal commitment to public good, and of a steadfast dedication to the principles of democracy. She presented herself as a leader ready not only to guide but also to serve, to not only speak but also to listen, and to not only govern but also to empower.

In the quiet moments of self-reflection, Ming-Na considered the full breadth of what her candidacy would entail. The public's eye was discerning, and the political arena was unforgiving. She committed herself to a regimen that would prepare her for every aspect of the campaign. Public speaking became a daily practice; she would stand before mirrors, refining her gestures and expressions, ensuring her message was conveyed with clarity and conviction.

Understanding that criticism is an inherent part of political life, Ming-Na sought to build a relationship with it. She engaged with critics, seeking to understand the root of their concerns, and using these interactions as opportunities to refine her platform. She recognized that not all criticism was constructive, but within the chaff, there was often a kernel of truth that could help her grow.

At the heart of stories like Ming-Na's is an unwavering desire to contribute to the public good. From small-town council members to national legislators, the spark that drives individuals towards elected service frequently originates from a deep-seated connection to their communities and an empathetic response to the challenges they witness. The motivations may vary—a desire to effectuate change, a response to a community in need, or the inspiration drawn from a leader who has made a tangible difference—but the underlying thread is a belief in the potential for government to be a positive force for change.

The path to elected office is rarely linear or prescriptive. It is carved out through community engagement, advocacy, and often years of behind-the-scenes work that may go unnoticed. Yet, this preparatory phase is crucial, as it lays the foundation upon which successful public service is built. It is during this time that future elected officials learn the art of listening deeply to their constituents, understanding their concerns, and envisioning policies that can address them.

For many, the decision to run for office is made at the intersection of personal conviction and professional duty. It is a decision that comes with the recognition of the sacrifices involved, including the surrender of privacy and the assumption of public scrutiny. Yet, these are accepted as part of the broader responsibility to steward the public's trust and work towards the common good.

This initial step into the realm of elected service is often marked by a blend of idealism and pragmatism. Aspiring officeholders must navigate the complexities of campaign logistics, fundraising, and public messaging, all while staying true to their core values and the promises they intend to keep. The act of campaigning itself becomes a testing ground for resilience and the ability to communicate effectively with a broad audience.

The stories of those who embark on this journey reveal the diverse tapestry of backgrounds that enrich the political landscape. They come from all walks of life, bringing with them their personal histories, professional expertise, and lived experiences that inform their perspectives on governance and policy. These narratives are essential, as they offer insights into the motivations that drive public servants and the personal sacrifices they make in their commitment to leadership.

The journey into elected office is both a personal and a collective one, where individual aspirations are channeled into public service. It is a journey that requires courage, conviction, and a steadfast dedication to the ideals of democracy. As these individuals step into the public arena, they carry with them the hopes and the will of the people, ready to shape the policies and the future of their communities.

12.2. Campaigns of Character: Authenticity on the Trail

In the realm of public service, where the quest for office is often mired in the quagmire of political gameplay, authenticity emerges as the North Star for a new breed of candidates. It is the unwavering commitment to genuine character that cements the bond between a leader and the electorate, turning the tide against the prevailing winds of skepticism that buffet the political landscape. When a campaign is rooted in this bedrock of authenticity, it transcends the banality of political maneuvering, transforming into a powerful narrative that resonates with the electorate's deepest aspirations and values.

In today's public service arena, the pursuit of elected office can too often descend into a complex battleground of strategic posturing, where authenticity is obscured by the fog of political one-upmanship. However, there emerges a vanguard of candidates for whom authenticity is not just a buzzword but the guiding principle of their political existence. These individuals understand that the essence of genuine leadership is not found in the superficial charm of crafted personas but in the raw and unvarnished truth of their being. It is this steadfast adherence to authenticity that forms an indelible link with the electorate, a bond of trust that stands resilient against the gales of doubt and disenchantment that have long eroded the public's faith in their representatives.

For such candidates, authenticity is not an act of convenience, donned and doffed like campaign buttons; it is a deeply entrenched trait that informs their every action, statement, and policy. It is the courage to remain congruent with one's beliefs and the integrity to uphold them, even when the tempest of political expediency threatens to sweep them aside. An authentic campaign eschews the mundane scripts of political performance and instead presents a narrative pulsating with the heartbeat of the community it seeks to serve.

This new epoch of candidates uses their campaigns as canvases to paint the stories of their lives, not in broad, impersonal strokes, but with the meticulous detail borne of lived experiences and shared endeavors. They step onto the campaign stage not as distant figures spouting rehearsed lines but as members of the community, with soil from the same earth under their fingernails and the same concerns echoing in their thoughts. Theirs is a campaign of depth, where every handshake is a silent vow of solidarity, every speech a mosaic of local voices, and every policy a chapter from the pages of their constituents' daily lives.

Such a campaign becomes more than a mere race for office; it is a pilgrimage towards a collective future. It is a commitment to carry the collective chorus of the electorate into the solemn halls of decision-making, ensuring that their voices are not just heard but are instrumental in shaping the policies that govern their lives. This approach to campaigning is a beacon of hope, a signal to the electorate that their values are mirrored in their leaders, and their aspirations are interwoven with the fabric of political intent.

A campaign founded on authenticity lays down the roots for a governance style that is not only reflective of the electorate's values but also responsive to their evolving needs. It promises a governance that is not aloof and disconnected but one that is accessible, understandable, and, most importantly, genuinely representative of the people it serves. Such campaigns herald the dawn of a political renaissance where the currency of authenticity yields dividends in the form of trust, engagement, and a renewed belief in the transformative power of public service.

The campaign trail is more than a path to political office; it is a crucible where the mettle of a candidate's life story is tested and displayed. Each step on this journey is a stitch in the intricate tapestry that is the public narrative of a potential leader. Candidates bring with them a quilt of experiences, each patch representing personal encounters and shared struggles, which collectively form a vision not just for their tenure, but for the legacy they hope to leave behind. This is a path that demands courage—not the fleeting bravery of a single bold act, but the enduring fortitude to remain steadfast to one's convictions amid the swirling political maelstrom.

For a candidate, this journey is an opportunity to forge profound connections with the electorate, connections rooted in a mutual understanding and a shared desire for a better tomorrow. It's about the kind of presence that transcends the physical; a mental and emotional engagement that acknowledges every handshake, every story shared at a town hall, every concern raised during a door-to-door encounter. These are not mere political transactions; they are the building blocks of a relationship built on trust and understanding, where the candidate not only listens but hears, not only responds but acts.

In this pursuit, the campaign trail morphs into a pilgrimage of purpose, where the candidate's narrative intertwines with those of the people they aspire to represent. This interlacing creates a robust and resilient connection, one that can withstand the challenges of governance and the oftentimes harsh realities of implementing change. The candidate's promise to carry the voices of their constituents into the halls of power is not merely rhetorical—it is a sacred vow to serve as the conduit for the myriad stories and experiences that make up the community's collective voice.

In such campaigns, the candidate's own life story becomes a reflective surface for the electorate to see their history and their hopes for the future. It is a narrative that continually evolves, enriched by each new encounter, each shared triumph, and every common challenge overcome. The candidate's story is not static; it is dynamic and woven from the diverse threads of the community, creating a vibrant and inclusive vision of the future that is as multifaceted as the electorate itself.

To maintain this level of genuineness, assembling a campaign team that reflects the ethos of the candidate is critical. Each member of this team becomes an ambassador of authenticity, embodying the values and vision of the campaign. They are the standard-bearers of the candidate's message, tasked with the sacred duty of ensuring that every action taken, every word spoken, and every policy formulated is a true extension of the candidate's guiding principles. This team is charged with safeguarding the campaign's authenticity against the pressures to conform to political expediency or to echo the hollow promises that too often characterize electoral contests.

The empirical evidence supporting the efficacy of authentic campaigns is compelling. Research published in the Social Science Quarterly demonstrates that authenticity in political messaging significantly correlates with a more engaged electorate, leading to higher voter turnout and robust grassroots activism.[75] Furthermore, insights from Political Behavior suggest that authenticity distinguishes candidates in saturated fields, enabling them to establish a genuine connection with voters and stand out in a crowded political arena.[76]

Campaigns of character represent more than the strategic quest to secure an electoral victory; they symbolize a commitment to win over the hearts and minds of the citizenry. They embody the quintessence of democracy, wherein politics is perceived not merely as a battleground for power but as a collective endeavor to foster

societal progress.

Through this journey, the candidate demonstrates a readiness to not just navigate but to lead through the tempest of political pressures, championing the will of the people over the cacophony of partisan noise. It is an odyssey that underscores the essence of democracy—where governance is not dictated by the few but directed by the voices of the many. The candidate pledges to carry these voices forward, ensuring they resonate where the decisions that shape lives and futures are made, thereby reinforcing the foundational principle that governance is of the people, by the people, and for the people.

12.3. From Pledges to Policy: Translating Promises into Action

Navigating the delicate transition from campaign promises to enacted policy is perhaps the most defining challenge for any elected official. This pivotal process of turning pledges into actionable policy is not merely an administrative task; it is the crucible in which the credibility of a leader and the trust of the public are continually tested and affirmed. It is within this dynamic interplay of promise and practice that the substance of a politician's commitment is realized and judged.

Public servants dedicated to transformational leadership must tread this path with a blend of bold vision and meticulous execution. The aspirational language that once captivated audiences must now be translated into the precise language of legislation and policy. The journey from the heady optimism of the campaign trail to the pragmatic corridors of power demands not just the ability to inspire but also the grit to implement. It requires a leader to harness the collective hope they have ignited and channel it into the mechanisms of governance.

A leader must wield the tools of vision and tactics in equal measure to navigate the complex web of legislative bureaucracy. The ideals that galvanized a community's support must now be tempered with the hard realities of political process and compromise. It is through this lens of practicality that the grand designs of electoral promises are distilled into the concrete steps of policy development and enactment. This delicate art of balance—preserving the essence of one's vision while adapting to the art of the possible—is the hallmark of effective governance.

In the realm of public service, the mantle of transformational leadership is not carried lightly. Those who step into this arena must do so armed with a bold vision that challenges the status quo, coupled with an unwavering commitment to see that vision through to fruition. The language that once painted pictures of a brighter future in the minds of the electorate must now be codified into the detailed statutes and actionable directives of governance. This evolution from the rousing crescendos of the campaign trail to the measured prose of policy is a testament to a leader's ability not only to dream but to do—to turn the tide of collective hope into the currents that power the engines of government.

Encouraging personal virtues such as honesty, diligence, and a sense of justice in public servants is crucial to this transformation. The call to public service is a call to embody these virtues, to become the standard-bearers of integrity and the exemplars of ethical leadership. In a landscape often marred by the shadows cast by those who fall short, it is essential to recognize and champion the quiet majority of public servants who serve with honor, often unnoticed. These individuals navigate the complexities of governance with a moral compass that points steadfastly towards the greater good, irrespective of the allure of shortcuts or the temptation to succumb to personal gain.

The narrative of public service is frequently skewed by the spotlight on the few who tarnish its image rather than the many who uphold its values. While the media's focus on the misconduct of dishonest politicians is a necessary function of a healthy democracy, ensuring accountability and transparency, it is equally important to highlight the dedication and integrity of the vast majority of public servants. Their stories, though less sensational, are the bedrock upon which the edifice of public trust is built. They are the unsung heroes who, day in and day out, do their utmost for the people they serve, often with little fanfare or recognition.

Journalists, in their role as watchdogs of democracy, perform the indispensable task of holding leaders accountable. This scrutiny is a vital component of the democratic process, ensuring that those in power remain answerable to those they represent. However, it is just as necessary to balance this scrutiny with acknowledgment of the positive impact made by public servants who embody the highest ideals of service. Their collective efforts are the threads that weave the fabric of a society that values integrity and rewards virtue.

The art of governance, therefore, is not just about maintaining a balance between vision and practicality but also about fostering an environment where personal virtues are not only encouraged but expected. It is about creating a culture in public service where integrity is the norm, not the exception. Leaders who can marry their aspirational rhetoric with the realities of policy-making, who can navigate the labyrinthine corridors of power without losing sight of their moral and ethical bearings, are the true champions of governance.

Effective governance emerges when these virtues are woven into the daily practice of policymaking, when each decision is infused with an awareness of its ethical implications, and when leaders act as stewards of the public's trust. By embracing the personal virtues that underpin their roles, public servants can ensure that the grand designs promised on the campaign trail are realized in the halls of governance with a clear conscience and a pure purpose. It is through their efforts that the noble calling of public service is redeemed and the faith of the electorate in their representatives is both justified and sustained.

The currency of a leader's word is their accountability to the electorate. In the post-election landscape, promises must be matched with progress, dreams with delivery. This entails a meticulous process of goal-setting, benchmarking, and transparent reporting. The leader must communicate not only the victories but also the inevitable setbacks and recalibrations that are part and parcel of the policy-making journey. It is in this ongoing dialogue with constituents that the integrity of a leader's intentions is continuously honed and evidenced.

In the intricate dance of democracy, the promises made by a leader are the steps they must remember long after the music of the campaign has faded. The transition from candidate to elected official marks a shift from aspiration to action, where the currency of their word is their unwavering accountability to those they serve. This transition is underpinned by a rigorous process of goal-setting, wherein ambitions are distilled into actionable objectives, and dreams are carefully mapped onto the tangible plane of policy and practice.

The art of leadership in this context becomes one of strategic orchestration, where each pledge is a note played in the grand symphony of governance. It is a meticulous process that requires not just the setting of goals but also the establishment of clear benchmarks against which progress can be measured. These benchmarks serve as the signposts that guide the electorate on the journey from rhetoric to reality, providing a clear line of sight to the destination promised.

Transparent reporting becomes the drumbeat to which a leader marches, providing a rhythm of reliability that constituents can trust. It is essential that leaders communicate with candor not only the milestones reached but also the hurdles encountered along the way. In doing so, they demonstrate a commitment to honesty that strengthens the bond with their constituency. This open discourse becomes a platform for collective reflection, an opportunity to recalibrate strategies in light of new challenges and to renew the collective resolve to move forward.

The ongoing dialogue between a leader and their constituents is a crucible in which the integrity of a leader's intentions is both refined and demonstrated. It is a conversation that must be rooted in a mutual pursuit of clarity and a shared commitment to seeing promises transformed into palpable outcomes. In this exchange, the leader's credibility is continuously forged, tested by the fire of public scrutiny and strengthened by the transparency of their actions.

The ultimate testament to a campaign's authenticity is the real-life impact of its policies. Each measure enacted, each reform introduced, stands as a tangible fulfillment of a campaign pledge, a brick laid in the edifice of a community's progress. This is where the narrative of an election becomes interwoven with the lived experience of the electorate, where the abstract becomes the actual, and where political legacy is cemented.

The journey from campaign to policy is marked by its complexity and demands a comprehensive commitment to the principles of public service and the pursuit of actionable progress. It is a narrative that not only educates and inspires but also challenges and motivates. It serves as a clarion call to all current and aspiring leaders that the path of political integrity is paved with the concrete achievements of policy that reflect the aspirations and address the needs of the people they serve. Through the shared experiences and strategies detailed herein, the reader is invited to contemplate the profound legacy of leadership that bridges the divide between promise and practice.

EPILOGUE

The Personal is Bureaucratic

The Interweaving of Personal Stories and Systemic Change

As this exploration of heart-led governance and its impact on the bureaucratic landscape draws to a close, we are compelled to reflect on the intricate dance between personal narratives and systemic change. The stories detailed within these pages—of individuals who have transformed the sterile corridors of government into conduits of empathy and innovation—serve as a testament to the profound influence that personal conviction can exert on the mechanisms of public service.

These narratives are not isolated chapters but are interwoven threads in the larger tapestry of bureaucratic evolution, highlighting a truth that has long been overlooked: the personal is not just political; it is bureaucratic. The aspirations and challenges of those who serve, their resilience in the face of adversity, and their unwavering commitment to the public good are the very fibers that strengthen the fabric of governance.

In this realm, where policies and lives intersect, the inclusion of personal experiences in policymaking does not undermine professionalism; instead, it enriches it, ensuring that the resultant policies are not only efficacious but also just and compassionate. These stories illustrate that when personal insights are integrated into the policymaking process, the resulting actions resonate more deeply with the populace, fostering trust and facilitating more meaningful engagement with the institutions that serve them.

Moreover, as these personal stories unfurl within the public sector, they challenge and inspire others to view their roles not as mere jobs but as opportunities to effect tangible change. They underscore the potential for every individual within the system to act as an agent of progress, leveraging their unique perspectives and experiences to foster innovation and drive reform.

The journey of intertwining personal narratives with systemic change is not without its challenges. It requires a cultural shift towards recognizing and valuing the diversity of experiences that public servants bring to their roles. It calls for a reimagining of leadership, one that is grounded in authenticity, empathy, and a willingness to engage with the multifaceted human elements that underpin governance.

This cultural shift is already underway, as evidenced by the stories shared throughout this text. From the halls of local government offices to the chambers of national policy, the ripple effects of this transformation are beginning to take shape. They can be seen in policies that more accurately reflect the complexities of the human condition, in public services that are more attuned to the needs they aim to meet, and in a renewed sense of camaraderie and purpose among those who dedicate their lives to public service.

As readers embark on their own journeys within the public sector, it is hoped that the narratives and insights contained herein will serve as a source of inspiration and guidance. The path forward is one of continued learning, adaptation, and growth—a journey that does not end with the final pages of this book but continues as each individual contributes their verse to the ongoing story of public service.

The intersection of personal stories and systemic change is where true transformation occurs. It is where the bureaucratic becomes personal, and the personal becomes bureaucratic. It is the nexus where the future of governance is being written, one story, one policy, one act of service at a time.

In this continued journey, the next steps are clear: to listen, to learn, and to lead with a heart that understands the weight of its responsibilities and the power of its influence. For in the end, it is the interweaving of the personal with the bureaucratic that will define the legacy of governance in our time—and it is a journey that we undertake together.

Next Steps: Continuing the Journey Beyond the Book

Embarking on the journey through the intricate world of government, we've unveiled the profound interplay between personal dedication and the overarching framework of public service. The unfolding of each narrative within these pages is not merely to inform but to spark a movement of purpose-driven transformation that each reader can carry forward. As the book draws to a close, the principles laid out become the compass for continued exploration and action in the vast ocean of governance.

For the readers stepping into the arena of public service, the commitment to imbue their work with the values of emotional intelligence becomes a mission. The challenge is to thread the needle of innovation through the dense fabric of bureaucracy, to embed integrity into the fabric of daily operations, and to approach ethical dilemmas with a blend of moral clarity and practical wisdom. The 'small wins' philosophy becomes a mantra, guiding them through the complex maze of red tape and into the clearings of impactful change.

Leaders who have traversed the pages of this book are summoned to a higher calling. They are entrusted with the task of crafting a vision for the future that is steeped in the well-being of every individual they serve. They are to be architects of a reality where systemic change is born out of a culture rich with empathy and grounded in an understanding that policy and practice are not just administrative acts but profoundly human endeavors.

Citizens, too, are beckoned to step beyond the traditional bounds of civic engagement. Armed with insights into the soul of bureaucracy, they are encouraged to advocate for policies that pulse with the vibrant needs of the community. It is their voice and their commitment to accountability that can reinforce the structures of governance with the strength of public trust and cooperation.

The narrative continues as a commitment to mindfulness and self-care becomes an essential part of the dialogue. It acknowledges that the vitality of public servants is the heartbeat of effective bureaucracy. The resources provided in the appendices are not mere addendums but critical tools to ensure the sustainability of those who dedicate their lives to public service.

Looking ahead, the path is one of collective ambition and shared responsibility. It is a reminder that innovation in governance is a collaborative endeavor, requiring a symphony of diverse voices and talents. The transformative power of personal stories woven into systemic change becomes a guiding principle for those walking the path of public service.

As we step beyond the scope of this text, the call to action remains vibrant and unwavering. It is a call to continue the journey with open hearts and minds, to weave the personal passions and experiences into the broader narrative of governance. It is through this interlacing of the personal and the bureaucratic that we can collectively craft a government that truly resonates with and for its people.

FURTHER RESOURCES AND ACKNOWLEDGMENTS

As we conclude this journey through the world of public service and governance, I'd like to extend my gratitude to the many individuals and organizations that have inspired and informed the contents of this book. In the spirit of continued learning and growth, I encourage readers who are seeking to deepen their understanding and skills in public service to explore additional resources.

One such invaluable resource is **theGovCoach.com**. This platform offers a wealth of information and guidance for those looking to plan, develop, or strengthen their careers in public service or other bureaucratic environments. Whether you are a budding public servant or a seasoned professional, **theGovCoach.com** provides insights and tools to help you navigate the complex landscape of government work and achieve your professional goals. Remember, the journey of public service is one of continuous learning and adaptation.

ENDNOTES

1   Eseonu, T. (2022). Street-level bureaucracy: dilemmas of the individual in public services. Administrative Theory &Amp; Praxis, 45(3), 259-261. https://doi.org/10.1080/10841806.2022.2141020

2   Osborne, S., Radnor, Z., & Nasi, G. (2012). A new theory for public service management? toward a (public) service-dominant approach. The American Review of Public Administration, 43(2), 135-158. https://doi.org/10.1177/0275074012466935

3   Nicoletti, G. and Scarpetta, S. (2003). Regulation, productivity and growth: oecd evidence. Economic Policy, 18(36), 9-72. https://doi.org/10.1111/1468-0327.00102

4   Levie, J. and Autio, E. (2011). Regulatory burden, rule of law, and entry of strategic entrepreneurs: an international panel study. Journal of Management Studies, 48(6), 1392-1419. https://doi.org/10.1111/j.1467-6486.2010.01006.x

5   Moore, W. and Frye, S. (2019). Review of hipaa, part 2: limitations, rights, violations, and role for the imaging technologist. Journal of Nuclear Medicine Technology, 48(1), 17-23. https://doi.org/10.2967/jnmt.119.227827

6   Shrivastava, B. and Dave, S. (2023). Gross national happiness. Climate Change Management and Social Innovations for Sustainable Global Organization, 175-194. https://doi.org/10.4018/978-1-6684-9503-2.ch012

7   Savitri, R., Cahyarini, B. R., Ahad, M. P. Y., Firmansyah, N., Gusparirin, R., & Samsara, L. (2023). Indonesian public service innovation trends: an analysis based on public service innovation competition top innovations 2014-2019. KnE Social Sciences. https://doi.org/10.18502/kss.v8i5.12995

8   Wright, B. E. (2007). Public service and motivation: does mission matter?. Public Administration Review, 67(1), 54-64. https://doi.org/10.1111/j.1540-6210.2006.00696.x

9   Ertas, N., "Public Service Motivation Theory and Voluntary Organizations," Nonprofit and Voluntary Sector Quarterly, 2012. doi:10.1177/0899764012459254. This article discusses the relationship between public service motivation and voluntary organizations, highlighting

that government employees engage in significantly more volunteering than their private-sector counterparts.

10 Zhong et al. "Public Service Delivery and the Livelihood Adaptive Capacity of Farmers and Herders: The Mediating Effect of Livelihood Capital" Land (2022) doi:10.3390/land11091467

11 Locke, E. A., & Latham, G. P. (2002). Building a practically useful theory of goal setting and task motivation: A 35-year odyssey. American Psychologist, 57(9), 705–717. doi:10.1037/0003-066X.57.9.705

12 Seabrooke, L. and Sending, O. J. (2022). Consultancies in public administration. Public Administration, 100(3), 457-471. https://doi.org/10.1111/padm.12844

13 Harris, A. S., Meyer-Sahling, J., Mikkelsen, K. S., Schuster, C., Seim, B., & Sigman, R. (2022). Varieties of connections, varieties of corruption: evidence from bureaucrats in five countries. Governance, 36(3), 953-972. https://doi.org/10.1111/gove.12714

14 Denhardt, J. V. and Denhardt, R. B. (2003). The new public service: serving, not steering. Choice Reviews Online, 40(09), 40-5440-40-5440. https://doi.org/10.5860/choice.40-5440

15 Boyne, G. (2001). planning, performance and public services. public Administration, 79(1), 73-88. https://doi.org/10.1111/1467-9299.00246

16 Eseonu, T. (2022). Street-level bureaucracy: dilemmas of the individual in public services. Administrative Theory &Amp; Praxis, 45(3), 259-261. https://doi.org/10.1080/10841806.2022.2141020

17 Brewer, G. A., Selden, S. C., & Facer, R. L. (2000). Individual conceptions of public service motivation. Public Administration Review, 60(3), 254-264. https://doi.org/10.1111/0033-3352.00085

18 Bowles, S. and Gintis, H. (2002). Social capital and community governance. The Economic Journal, 112(483), F419-F436. https://doi.org/10.1111/1468-0297.00077

19 Chen, C. and Hsieh, C. (2015). Knowledge sharing motivation in the public sector: the role of public service motivation. International Review of Administrative Sciences, 81(4), 812-832. https://doi.org/10.1177/0020852314558032

20 Olsen, J. P. (2005). Maybe it is time to rediscover bureaucracy. Journal of Public Administration Research and Theory, 16(1), 1-24. https://doi.org/10.1093/jopart/mui027

21 Herrigel, G. (2020). Experimentalist systems in manufacturing multinationals: recursivity and continuous learning through destabilization. Knowledge for Governance, 415-439. https://doi.org/10.1007/978-3-030-47150-7_18

22 Gatenby, M., Rees, C., Truss, C., Alfes, K., & Soane, E. (2014). Managing change, or changing managers? the role of middle managers in uk public service reform. Public Management Review, 17(8), 1124-1145. https://doi.or g/10.1080/14719037.2014.895028

23 Andersson, T., Stockhult, H., & Tengblad, S. (2020). Strategies for co-workership retention. Human Resource Development International, 24(4), 425-445. https://doi.org/10.1080/13678868.2020.1840845

24 Ray, A. (2015). The body keeps the score: brain, mind, and body in the healing of trauma. The Permanente Journal, 19(3). https://doi.org/10.7812/tpp/14-211

25 Hernandez-Wolfe, P., Killian, K. D., Engström, D., & Gangsei, D. (2014). Vicarious resilience, vicarious trauma, and awareness of equity in trauma work. Journal of Humanistic Psychology, 55(2), 153-172. https://doi. org/10.1177/0022167814534322

26 Kalshoven, K. and Boon, C. (2012). Ethical leadership, employee well-being, and helping. Journal of Personnel Psychology, 11(1), 60-68. https://doi. org/10.1027/1866-5888/a000056

27 Havaei, F., Adhami, N., Tang, X., Boamah, S. A., Kaulius, M., Gubskaya, E., ... & O'Donnell, K. (2023). Workplace predictors of violence against nurses using machine learning techniques: a cross-sectional study utilizing the national standard of psychological workplace health and safety. Healthcare, 11(7), 1008. https://doi.org/10.3390/healthcare11071008

28 Gordon, V. (2016). Emotional labor: putting the service in public service. Public Voices, 12(2), 108. https://doi.org/10.22140/pv.93

29 Riforgiate, S. E., Howes, S. S., & Simmons, M. J. (2021). The impact of daily emotional labor on health and well-being. Management Communication Quarterly, 36(3), 391-417. https://doi.org/10.1177/08933189211041352

30 Johnson, H. M. and Spector, P. E. (2007). Service with a smile: do emotional intelligence, gender, and autonomy moderate the emotional labor process?. Journal of Occupational Health Psychology, 12(4), 319-333. https://doi. org/10.1037/1076-8998.12.4.319

31 Sloan, M. M. (2012). The consequences of emotional labor for public sector workers and the mitigating role of self-efficacy. The American Review of Public Administration, 44(3), 274-290. https://doi.org/10.1177/0275074012462864

32 Pandey, J. (2018). Managing emotional labor for service employees: an hrm-based approach. Human Resource Management International Digest, 26(4), 1-4. https://doi.org/10.1108/hrmid-04-2017-0072

33 Gordon, V. (2016). Emotional labor: putting the service in public service. Public Voices, 12(2), 108. https://doi.org/10.22140/pv.93

34 GGI Insights. (2023, August 30). Em https://chat.openai.com/c/ cb9d2606-5a9f-410f-a89d-686f8eb942dcotional Intelligence: Unlocking the EQ Code. Gray Group International. Retrieved from

35 Clark, M. A., Michel, J. S., Zhdanova, L., Pui, S. Y., & Baltes, B. B. (2019). "I feel your pain": A critical review of organizational research on empathy. Journal of Organizational Behavior, 40(2), 166-196. doi:10.1002/job.2348

36 Goleman, D., Boyatzis, R. E., & McKee, A. (2002). Primal leadership: realizing the power of emotional intelligence. Choice Reviews Online, 40(01), 40-0392-40-0392. https://doi.org/10.5860/choice.40-0392

37 Edlins, M. (2019). Developing a model of empathy for public administration. Administrative Theory &Amp; Praxis, 43(1), 22-41. https://doi.org/10.1080 /10841806.2019.1700459

38 Lu, X., Lee, H. J., Yang, S., & Song, M. K. (2020). The dynamic role of emotional intelligence on the relationship between emotional labor and job satisfaction: a comparison study of public service in china and south korea. Public Personnel Management, 50(3), 356-380. https://doi. org/10.1177/0091026020946476

39 (2001). The benefits of interventions for work-related stress. American Journal of Public Health, 91(2), 270-276. https://doi.org/10.2105/ajph.91.2.270

40 Sloan, M. (2012). The consequences of emotional labor for public sector workers and the mitigating role of self-efficacy. The American Review of Public Administration, 44(3), 274-290. https://doi.org/10.1177/0275074012462864

41 Halliday, S., Burns, N., Hutton, N., McNeill, F., & Tata, C. (2009). Street-level bureaucracy, interprofessional relations, and coping mechanisms: a study of criminal justice social workers in the sentencing process. Law &Amp; Policy, 31(4), 405-428. https://doi.org/10.1111/j.1467-9930.2009.00306.x

42 Ong, A. D., Bergeman, C. S., Bisconti, T. L., & Wallace, K. A. (2006). Psychological resilience, positive emotions, and successful adaptation to stress in later life. Journal of Personality and Social Psychology, 91(4), 730–749. doi:10.1037/0022-3514.91.4.730

43 Fischer et al. "Stress Reduction by Yoga versus Mindfulness Training in Adults Suffering from Distress: A Three-Armed Randomized Controlled Trial including Qualitative Interviews (RELAX Study)" Journal of clinical medicine (2022)

44 HBR. (2022, June). The Power of Healthy Relationships at Work. Harvard Business Review. https://hbr.org/2022/06/the-power-of-health y-relationships-at-work

45 Obrist, B., Pfeiffer, M., Henley, R., & Robert, W. (2010). Multi-layered social resilience. Progress in Development Studies. doi:10.1177/

146499340901000402. Available at: https://www.ncbi.nlm.nih.gov/pmc/articles/PMC6402129/

46 Smyth, J. M., & Pennebaker, J. W. (2008). Exploring the boundary conditions of expressive writing: In search of the right recipe. British Journal of Health Psychology, 13(1), 1-7. doi:10.1348/135910707X250300

47 Wright, T. and Huang, C. (2012). The many benefits of employee well-being in organizational research. Journal of organizational Behavior, 33(8), 1188-1192. https://doi.org/10.1002/job.1828

48 Shier, M. L. and Turpin, A. (2021). Trauma-informed organizational dynamics and client outcomes in concurrent disorder treatment. Research on Social Work Practice, 32(1), 92-105. https://doi.org/10.1177/10497315211013908

49 Douglas "Mitigating workplace adversity through employee resilience" Strategic hr review (2020)

50 Purtle, J. (2018). Systematic review of evaluations of trauma-informed organizational interventions that include staff trainings. Trauma, Violence, &Amp; Abuse, 21(4), 725-740. https://doi.org/10.1177/1524838018791304

51 Walle, S. (2017). Explaining citizen satisfaction and dissatisfaction with public services., 227-241. https://doi.org/10.1057/978-1-137-55269-3_11

52 Walle, S. (2017). Explaining citizen satisfaction and dissatisfaction with public services., 227-241. https://doi.org/10.1057/978-1-137-55269-3_11

53 Rodrigues, N., Ham, E., Kirsh, B., Seto, M., & Hilton, N. (2021). Mental health workers' experiences of support and help-seeking following workplace violence: a qualitative study. Nursing and Health Sciences, 23(2), 381-388. https://doi.org/10.1111/nhs.12816

54 Edwards JP, Solomon PL. Explaining job satisfaction among mental health peer support workers. Psychiatr Rehabil J. 2023 Sep;46(3):223-231. doi: 10.1037/prj0000577. Epub 2023 Jul 20. PMID: 37470983.

55 Bhide, A. (1996). The Questions Every Entrepreneur Must Answer. Harvard Business Review. Retrieved from https://hbr.org/1996/11/the-questions-every-entrepreneur-must-answer

56 Sørensen, E. and Torfing, J. (2011). Enhancing collaborative innovation in the public sector. Administration &Amp; Society, 43(8), 842-868. https://doi.org/10.1177/0095399711418768

57 Cordella, A. and Paletti, A. (2019). Government as a platform, orchestration, and public value creation: the italian case. Government Information Quarterly, 36(4), 101409. https://doi.org/10.1016/j.giq.2019.101409

58 Shanahan, E. A., Jones, M. D., & McBeth, M. K. (2010). A Narrative Policy Framework: Clear Enough to Be Wrong? Policy Studies Journal, 38(2), 329-353. doi:10.1111/j.1541-0072.2010.00364.x

59 Sørensen, E. and Torfing, J. (2011). Enhancing collaborative innovation in the public sector. Administration &Amp; Society, 43(8), 842-868. https://doi.org/10.1177/0095399711418768

60 Tavares, A. F., Pires, S. M., & Teles, F. (2021). Voice, responsiveness, and alternative policy venues: an analysis of citizen complaints against the local government to the national ombudsman. Public Administration, 100(4), 1054-1072. https://doi.org/10.1111/padm.12787

61 Al-Mawali, H. and Al-Busaidi, K. A. (2021). Knowledge sharing through enterprise social media in a telecommunications context. International Journal of Knowledge Management, 18(1), 1-27. https://doi.org/10.4018/ijkm.291706

62 Kerr, R., Garvin, J., Heaton, N., & Boyle, E. (2006). Emotional intelligence and leadership effectiveness. Leadership &Amp; Organization Development Journal, 27(4), 265-279. https://doi.org/10.1108/01437730610666028

63 Porath, C., & Boissy, A. (2023, February 10). Practice Empathy as a Team. Harvard Business Review. Retrieved from https://hbr.org/2023/02/practice-empathy-as-a-team

64 Arghode, V., Lathan, A., Alagaraja, M., Rajaram, K., & McLean, G. N. (2021). Empathic organizational culture and leadership: conceptualizing the framework. European Journal of Training and Development, 46(1/2), 239-256. https://doi.org/10.1108/ejtd-09-2020-0139

65 Furman, J. L., Porter, M. E., & Stern, S. (2002). The determinants of national innovative capacity. Research Policy, 31(6), 899-933. https://doi.org/10.1016/s0048-7333(01)00152-4

66 Furman, J. L., Porter, M. E., & Stern, S. (2002). The determinants of national innovative capacity. Research Policy, 31(6), 899-933. https://doi.org/10.1016/s0048-7333(01)00152-4

67 Barbuto, J. E. and Wheeler, D. W. (2006). Scale development and construct clarification of servant leadership. Group &Amp; Organization Management, 31(3), 300-326. https://doi.org/10.1177/1059601106287091

68 U.S. Environmental Protection Agency. (2017). Digital Strategy. Retrieved from https://19january2017snapshot.epa.gov/open/digital-strategy_.html.

69 U.S. Environmental Protection Agency. (n.d.). Digital Strategy. Retrieved from https://www.epa.gov/developers/digital-strategy.

70 Homberg, F., McCarthy, D., & Tabvuma, V. (2015). A meta-analysis of the relationship between public service motivation and job satisfaction. Public Administration Review, 75(5), 711-722. https://doi.org/10.1111/puar.12423

71 Issah, M. (2021). Perception of fit and job satisfaction among administrative staff in a mid-western university in the united states of america. Sage Open, 11(2), 215824402110275. https://doi.org/10.1177/21582440211027564

72 Homberg, F., McCarthy, D., & Tabvuma, V. (2015). A meta-analysis of the relationship between public service motivation and job satisfaction. Public Administration Review, 75(5), 711-722. https://doi.org/10.1111/puar.12423

73 Issah, M. (2021). Perception of fit and job satisfaction among administrative staff in a mid-western university in the united states of america. Sage Open, 11(2), 215824402110275. https://doi.org/10.1177/21582440211027564

74 Allen, T. D., Eby, L. T., Poteet, M. L., Lentz, E., & Lima, L. (2004). Career benefits associated with mentoring for proteges: a meta-analysis.. Journal of Applied Psychology, 89(1), 127-136. https://doi.org/10.1037/0021-9010.89.1.127

75 Hogan, R. (2012). campaign spending and voter participation in state legislative elections. Social Science Quarterly, 94(3), 840-864. https://doi.org/10.1111/j.1540-6237.2012.00897.x

76 Stiers, D., Larner, J., Kenny, J., Breitenstein, S., Vallée-Dubois, F., & Lewis-Beck, M. (2019). candidate authenticity: 'to thine own self be true'. Political Behavior, 43(3), 1181-1204. https://doi.org/10.1007/s11109-019-09589-y

Printed in the United States
by Baker & Taylor Publisher Services